Australian Aboriginal Women's Autobiographies

A Critical Study

Australian Aboriginal Women's Autobiographies

A Critical Study

SUNEETHA RANI

Prestige

an international publishing house

Published by
Prestige Books
3/28, East Patel Nagar
New Delhi 110 008
Ph. 9818755529
Prestigebooks@gmail.com
ISBN: 81-7551-179-6

Printed at Chaman Offset Press, New Delhi 110 002

Contents

Introduction

The present study proposes to assess the nature and contribution of Australian Aboriginal women's autobiographies in English. It will attempt to describe and evaluate major trends of content and representation in them as well as their integration of the form of autobiography to their cultural-political situation and purposes. Around the periphery of this field, the study will attempt to place these autobiographies within the context of Australian Aboriginal literature.

Australian Aboriginal literature in English comprises a variety of works in all genres and styles. It also represents a variety of attitudes to the Aboriginal situation, urging us to approach it cautiously to avoid the common errors arising from over-generalisation. For example, in her article "One Aboriginal Woman's Identity: Walking in Both Worlds," Lillian Holt begins her discourse with a warning that provides an introduction to Aboriginal women's writing. She is strong in her denial of the assumption that one Aboriginal woman writer writes for all women:

> No, I am not speaking on behalf of all Aboriginal people, or all Aboriginal women. We are not a homogeneous group. This needs to be said because often Aboriginal people are burdened by the expectation that any one of us can be a "spokesperson" for our whole race. Taken to its extreme, such an expectation means that if one Aborigine fouls up, the whole race gets the label. So I make this plain at the beginning: I speak for myself and I speak from the experience of being an Aboriginal woman in this country called Australia. (175)

Holt's words introduce readers of Aboriginal literature to a world of debates, discussions, controversies, traumas and assertions, and most of all to differences, and to the need to avoid glossing over differences. Apart from all these, the above statement reminds us of facts in the history and lives of the Aboriginal people of Australia. Aborigines, as Holt says, were not a homogeneous group. Before colonisation they comprised numerous tribes, spread all over Australia, with different languages and different cultures.

Colonised Australia, however, does present a very grim picture of Aboriginal people in general. They are in a minority in their own land and many Aboriginal tribes and most languages have, in fact, become extinct. Land, sacred to Aboriginals, has been lost to the colonisers. Only their Aboriginal consciousness keeps them united in this predicament in spite of their differences in language, culture, colour, region and religion. It is also this unity that makes them fight, at times with a martial spirit, against discrimination and motivates them to assert their Aboriginal identity.

In his book *Living Black*, Kevin Gilbert says, "White people's devaluation of Aboriginal life, religion, culture and personality caused the thinking about self and race that I believe is the key to modern Aboriginal thinking" (1978: 2). Similarly, Adam Shoemaker says that a fundamental relationship exists between the sociopolitical milieu and Aboriginal creative writing in English. He reasserts his view by further saying that black creative writing cannot be studied in isolation and that it must be examined and evaluated in terms of the social environment which surrounds it and the historical events which precede it (Shoemaker 6). Both Gilbert and Shoemaker construct a context to meet, understand and interpret Aboriginal literature. These statements implicitly suggest the rise of Aboriginal literature from Aboriginal suffering and Aboriginal activism. Aboriginal literature springs from such depths of experience that without an introduction to history and culture it becomes impossible to interpret it.

At the same time, as will be discussed in the second chapter of this book, Aboriginal literature also adopts strategies of deliberate silence over certain issues, almost as a means of holding power in hand. It is interesting to look at various arguments about Aboriginal literature being the outcome of Aboriginal suffering. For instance, in a cautionary tone Stephen Muecke says, in "Aboriginal Literature and the Repressive Hypothesis," that the "repressive hypothesis"

> is one such framing which I have rejected because it is burdened by a Romantic legacy of the expressive self. It would say that Aboriginal literature is the psychological outcome of social oppression. . . . Authenticity, problematic as it is for many reasons, is a necessary part of the formula which produces the repressive hypothesis. (405)

But it is also important to see the variety of opinion Aboriginal creative writers themselves have held about their writings, for they have held and expressed diverse views about themes, intention and inspiration of their works. For instance, Melissa Lucashenko does not see Aboriginal writing as a distinct body of work, but more as an issue of content: "Aboriginal writing to me at the moment is a protest literature I suppose and it's centred around land and social justice and legal stuff" (Ruffo 212).

Although she says that Aboriginal literature is a protest literature, Lucashenko does not rule out the possibility of other themes. Similarly, other motives also co-exist in the shaping of contemporary Aboriginal literature, as we understand from Mudrooroo's observation that

> over the last decades conditions have improved and with this improvement Indigenous literature has begun to turn towards cultural and self introspection. Guilt and blame are not enough for the continuation of a literature and so histories from an Indigenous viewpoint are being constructed; life stories (often in collaboration), novels, short stories and poems are devoting their words to the Indigenous existential being in what is now said to be a 'multicultural' Australia and what in a few years' time will be a republican Australia. (Mudrooroo 1997: 3)

Hence, we may say that an Aboriginal literary discourse emerges from the Aboriginal suffering as the new history (in the short or the longer term) of colonised people expressing themselves in the language of the coloniser. However, Aboriginal writers do adopt strategies of shaping this history by selective disclosure. Yet, although most Aboriginal literature deals with the colonial predicament, it is not confined to the coloniser-colonised discourse alone. For example, in a personal interview with Adam Shoemaker, Mona

Tur, who writes under her tribal name of Ngitji Ngitji, says, "I'm not one for political things. I get most of my poetry through nature" (Shoemaker 221). But she admits that she is aware of the fact that politics and life go together and that she responds in the form of poetry to atrocities on Aborigines.

Aboriginal literature functions as an introduction to the people's history and present predicament, and as an eye-opener to non-Aboriginal people. Refusing to fit automatically into any western intellectual discourse, Aboriginal literature emerges as a decolorised/decolonising literature in its spirit, content, purpose and functions. This literature functions not only as literature, but also as a historical, social, political and economic discourse, and it also inevitably bends the English language. Anne Brewster rightly observes that by reclaiming and rewriting history, Aboriginal women intend educating both black and white Australians:

> For white Australians this education has the purpose of revealing the violence of colonisation which has been suppressed in official histories. For Aboriginal people the narration of the past has the additional role of producing a sense of unity and group solidarity. The awareness of a common past can thus bind together people who have been dispossessed. (1996: 53-54)

Aboriginal literature emerges as a multidimensional and interdisciplinary discourse as it explores and recreates the Aboriginal situation of both today and the past. At times, it seems to consider the validity of the linear classification of Aboriginal life into past, present and future phases of time. In her article "Chasing an Identity: An Aboriginal Perspective on Aboriginality," Nellie Green says: "It is the Aboriginal way of thinking to respect that the past is as much of the future as it is the past" (Reed-Gilbert 52). Although their original concepts of time are different from the western concept of linear time, Aboriginal writers do divide time in order to address three important sequential phases in Aboriginal history: the first phase is the Aboriginal past before the advent of whites in Australia; the present, extended over the past two hundred years and standing for the colonial situation; the future as the most powerful phase of Aboriginal life, for Aboriginal writers envisage a future which will be constructed by subverting the present and, wherever possible, reverting to the lost Aboriginal glory. Especially, Aboriginal spirituality raises the question of whether or not, or even how, to return to the "traditional" Aboriginal lifestyle and a pre-colonial or non-colonial state. Aboriginal writers look in the direction of Aboriginal spirituality for a redressal of their suffering. For the crucial practical question of turning towards a co-existence with the mainstream society on the basis of liberty and equality fails to address the inner being. Again, to quote Anne Brewster, what she says about Sally Morgan's *My Place* applies just as well to spirituality in contemporary Aboriginal people: "We can see that this spirituality is hybrid and draws not only on visions of the past and traditional Aboriginal culture, such as the Aboriginal music from the swamp, but also on Christian imagery" (1996: 27).

Mudrooroo compares Australia to a Grandfather Tree in whose shade many smaller trees and shrubs grow. This metaphor aptly identifies the ideal. For he hopes for a new, just and peaceful nation that still values indigenous ideals, of caring and sharing, of putting old wrongs aside and concentrating on the future. He demands that the majority group should negotiate with indigenous people as equals rather than imposing solutions on them. Regarding the question of spirituality, and the Aboriginal hope for their future, he says:

> It is rarely acknowledged that indigenous people were not the passive victims of an overwhelming advanced civilisation in the face of which their beliefs and customs simply crumbled away. This is a racist belief which needs challenging, for there is ample evidence that resistance to cultural domination from indigenous people was intense and that in response to the missionary impact they consciously modified their beliefs. Many of them did not become Christians, but succeeded in accommodating their beliefs to the new Christianity. (Mudrooroo 2001: 45-46)

Thus, by deconstructing the history of Aboriginal spirituality in its confrontation with colonial experience, Mudrooroo suggests, we can make room for an ideal future in which spirituality will play a significant part.

In his attempt to reconstruct history and visualise the future, he comes across to us as a committed Aboriginal historian as well. It is not out of place to quote here his classification of Aboriginal past in order to contextualise the Aboriginal situation as the Aboriginal people may see it. This classification of Aboriginal history is as follows (Mudrooroo 1997: 5):

1. The Time of the Dreaming: From the Beginning to 1788; Pre-history. Before the coming of the Europeans.
2. The Time of the Invasion(s): A convenient cutoff date for this period might be 1901 and the coming into being of the federation of the Australian colonies.
3. Punitive Expeditions and Protection: The utter conquering and control of Indigenous peoples with the framing of restrictive legislation.
4. The Colonial Period: Paternalism, then Assimilation: A convenient cutoff date is 1967 when a referendum was conducted which made Indigenous people Australian citizens.
5. The Period of Self-determination and Self-management: The official policy from 1967 to 1988.
6. The Period of Reconciliation: Sharing cultures.

Australian literature, and even the social sciences, seem to participate at times in the attempt to prove Australia a "terra nullius." Early Australian literature which describes Australia as a new and uninhabited land is an example of this. Even when the Aboriginal presence was acknowledged, it was either exorcised or condemned. The portrayal of indigenous people ranged from omission to overstatement. For instance, the concept terra nullius, the theory that Australia was uninhabited and unowned before Captain Cook stepped on its coast in 1770 (Horton 1994). A part of white Australia considers only this two hundred year old history. Yet many loopholes, pitfalls, absences and degradations arise from or are condoned by this view. But for Aboriginal people, who had to prove in the court of law that Australia was inhabited if not owned by Aboriginal people before the advent of whites, the past is the glorious Aboriginal past. This glorious past, according to Aboriginal writers, relates to a life of rich culture and heritage, stemming from close association with land, nature and liberty. Such literature as existed during this period was, of course, purely oral. Several factors played a crucial role, thereafter, in partial elimination and distortion of Aboriginal oral literature. Some of these factors will be discussed in the present chapter. For orality becomes a significant aspect of our subject alongside awareness of the past, as it is virtually impossible to dissociate the sense of a "speaking self" from autobiography.

Distortion of oral literature during the process of colonisation did not, fortunately, lead to its complete elimination. As Stephen Muecke observes in his article "Aboriginal Literature—Oral,"

> Aboriginal "Oral Literature" is alive and well . . . its response to colonialism was not one of acquiescence, but one of fighting back with words, making stories in order to come to terms with the structure of colonial economy and law and the place Aborigines were supposed to occupy in it; of articulating suffering; of satirising the various figures of the colonial administration and the pastoral industry. (Hergenhan 28)

This oral literature, which has thousands of years of history, lives today in the form of reconstructions in narratives of myths, tales, legends and songs. However, much of it now exists in English and operates as influence on written literature, again in English. It is not just Aboriginal spirituality that fought against the coloniser's religion; oral literature fought against it too. While Aboriginal spirituality accommodated some aspects of Christianity without losing itself, oral literature fought against colonisation with words, even as it adopted, eventually, the coloniser's language and literary forms.

A significant proportion of contemporary Aboriginal literature takes its cue from the Aboriginal oral tradition. It is thus influenced by both colonial and native traditions and forms. For instance, anthologies of Aboriginal writings such as *FROM OUR HEARTS: An Anthology of New Aboriginal Writing from Southwest Western Australia* (Kapetas 2000) and *The Strength of Us as Women: Black Women Speak* (Reed-Gilbert 2000) prove how firmly Aboriginal literature is rooted in its oral tradition and how strongly the Aboriginal writers have continued the oral tradition, although the form and the language have, of course, been modified. When the qualities of oral literature present in contemporary Aboriginal literature are mentioned, immediately women writers like Lisa Bellear, Anita Heiss and Ruby Langford Ginibi come to our mind, apart from many other prominent or less well-known writers. For instance, let us look at the poem "Long Ago" by Rosemary Plummer:

Long ago
there lived
an old woman
with a kangaroo bone
through her nose
She was wise
foremost of others
in various ceremonies
The people
of the tribe
called her Mukku Jangu. (Reed-Gilbert 24)

The poem goes on to describe the "old" woman's lifestyle and capabilities. The storytelling mode, simple diction, spontaneity of feeling and the theme of the poem all echo the oral tradition and the poet's commitment to it. The poem not only depicts an Aboriginal situation but also embodies an Aboriginal mode of articulation, except that it is written in the English language. In her book *Literary Formations: Post-Colonialism, Nationalism, Globalism* (1995), Anne Brewster points out the essential qualities of oral literature, such as direct address, telling as opposed to scripting, and the strong or manifest, assumed presence of a listener. She also finds other works such as Evelyn Crawford's *Over My Tracks: A Remarkable Life* (1993) akin to the Aboriginal oral tradition.

This tradition seems to be quite strong particularly in women's autobiographies, for like the tradition of storytelling, to which they are closely related, autobiographies also aim to record events, experiences and feelings for "direct"-sounding transmission, and to help in constructing histories; the spontaneity, the intimacy and identity with the experience mark them strongly with properties associated with oral narration. For instance, Joan Newman argues that in Sally Morgan's *My Place*, "A primary concern for the author was to achieve a successful integration of the oral aspects of the narrative and her own written testimony. This unity is particularly desirable in a narrative whose thematic concern is a unity between the narrator and her Aboriginal heritage" (Newman 1988: 380). She goes on to argue that the narrative use of the bird-call, for instance, operates powerfully at both a literate and an oral level since the origins of the sign of impending death are oral and folkloric, even though the form may be written. Mudrooroo also puts this idea across clearly when he says,

> Indigenous literature has been and often still is an oral discourse with different devices, such as absence of closure, narrative dominance, epic style, collective authorship and recitation, generic fluidity, repetition, non-verbal and semi-verbal markers and other devices which are often edited out when the literary text becomes an artifact to be read rather than heard. (1997: 57)

The Aboriginal "present," if the term is considered in a larger sense as the period after colonisation, is the gloomiest part of Aboriginal life. It is full of discrimination, ill-treatment and degradation, loss of land, people, culture, language and religion, and natural surroundings. While Aboriginals speak with nostalgia about their pre-colonial past, they speak with fear, hatred and protest concerning the colonial and post-colonial present. Memories of trauma and turmoil, massacre and violence at both physical and deeper levels dominate this period. This present has accommodated both the current reality and the stories of earlier alienation, elimination and even extermination of Aboriginal people. This present has, significantly, also witnessed the tumultuous struggle of Aboriginal people for survival and preservation of identity in white-dominated and racially discriminating society. In this struggle, the works of the authors we have chosen to study play an important role, even as they highlight a neglected aspect of this subject, the women's representation of their own predicament.

For this appreciation we need to recount, at least briefly, the history of colonisation. James Cook (1728-79) reached eastern Australia from New Zealand aboard the *Endeavour* on 19 April 1770, first sighting land at Point Hills in what is today's Victoria. His name became a short-hand term for theft in Aboriginal tales later on. He had his first face-to-face contact with Aborigines on 29

April at Botany Bay. The very first meeting resulted in Cook's firing at them to threaten them, peppering with light shot the legs of one man who then picked up a shield to defend himself (Horton 1994). The two sides of this story in a way anticipate the subsequent centuries of colonisation and resistance. Henry Reynolds' *Fate of a Free People: A Radical Re-Examination of the Tasmanian Wars* (1995) provides a detailed record of the European colonisation and native resistance, for instance the Black War (1824-1831), in Tasmania. In his Introduction to the book, Henry Reynolds notes:

> Identifying themselves as Aborigines, community members provided the springboard for the modern Aboriginal rights movement which emerged in the 1970s—a development which surprised many Tasmanians of European descent, who had been taught to believe that the island Aborigines had disappeared a hundred years earlier. (5)

The notion that Tasmanian Aborigines had been totally wiped out was, thus, given the lie.

The invaders/settlers also made friendship agreements with Aboriginal leaders at other times and in other places. There were other factors leading to the fresh burden placed on the Aboriginal people. Convicts were deported to Australia from over-populated eighteenth-century England. Prison houses were constructed in Australia. The dwellers of these also gradually turned into settlers, in addition to other settler-colonisers. In the name of friendship agreements too, in fact, land was "legally" snatched away from Aboriginal people. Indigenous culture, language, religion and freedom were also severely threatened with elimination by these forces, as by newer institutions such as reserves, missions, dormitories and the policy of separating children from parents. Thereafter, naturally, the Aboriginal people remained alienated outsiders in their own land.

A number of Aboriginal people, including children, were massacred during early colonisation. Women were sexually exploited, raped, abused, tormented and subjugated. Flour and water holes were poisoned, Aborigines were buried alive, and were tied to trees for shooting practice. Blankets used by people suffering from deadly diseases in London were distributed among the Aboriginal people. Terrible venereal diseases were transported into their midst by whites. Contacts between whites and Aboriginals led to complex situations of miscegenation. In the name of reform and education, mixed-blood children were, against all natural laws, removed from their Aboriginal parents. The Australian government believed that since mixed-blood children had white blood in them, they could be reformed and made into "human beings," unlike full-bloods, who were, they believed, beyond reformation. For the same "reason," Aboriginal parents were not considered fit to look after them. This entire "stolen generation" grew up in missionary dormitories to become domestics in white households or to suffer worse fate. Many full-blood Aboriginal people were already serving whites in virtual slavery. Mixed blood children eventually came to be called half-castes, quarter-castes and coloured people, accepted neither by Aboriginals nor by white people, thus becoming double-outcastes.

By means of such destructive mechanisms, the Aboriginal population in Queensland, for instance, had reduced from an estimated 120,000 in the 1820s to less than 20,000 by the 1920s. This reveals that Aboriginal society was being systematically and ruthlessly dismantled (L.R. Smith 122). Raymond Evans unveils the fact that this aspect of Australian history continued even after such practices were legally forbidden:

> Although children can no longer forcibly be taken from black parents by police protectors and missionaries under the Aborigines Protection Act, institutional control over black lives, police violence against blacks, poverty, malnutrition, disease, worsening alcoholism, educational and occupational discrimination, substandard housing and persistently virulent strains of white racism remain constant features in the daily lives of Queensland Aborigines. (19)

The twentieth century, thus, not only witnessed some of the landmarks in the history of white colonisation but also in the Aboriginal movement of protest and self-assertion. The Aborigines Act of 1905 had made the removal of Aboriginal children legally acceptable. These "wards of the state" had no rights under white law and any resistance to this absence of status was put down firmly, even vehemently, by the white government. However, the subsequent century also witnessed the assertion of Aboriginal identity and self-determination. Aboriginal people began to force their way into official Australian history and mainstream life as a people with definite aims and objectives. It was, simultaneously, the time of the rise of a modern Aboriginal literature, distinct from mere collections of traditional myths, and with a certain new consciousness of Aboriginality and approaches to consideration of Aboriginal identity. Naturally, this movement took many long decades to consolidate, to be noticed, and to achieve noteworthy results.

The 1960s, especially, saw the emergence, resurgence and strengthening of Aboriginal political movements. It was the result of action groups lobbying for recognition of Aboriginal rights. Aboriginal literature reflected this new mood as well. The white government's calls for assimilation and reconciliation were interpreted by some as a policy of division, of seeking to alienate individual Aborigines from their communities, of pushing them into white society, only to be dislocated, dispossessed and discriminated against. The Civil Rights Movement led to the 1967 referendum that finally allowed Aborigines to vote. Only in 1967 were Aborigines "granted" citizenship status in their own land. The Aboriginal Arts Board was established to enable aspiring Aboriginal artists to publish their work. The Mabo case was a remarkable milestone in Aboriginal history, for it attempted to restore Aboriginal land rights in Australia. Mabo was the Chair of the Torres Strait Border Action Committee in Townsville and had always been active in defending the Torres Strait Islanders' rights. In 1982, he and four other Torres Strait Islanders began legal proceedings to establish traditional ownership of their land in the Queensland Supreme Court and the High Court of Australia. In 1992, four months after Mabo's death due to cancer, judgement was given in favour of Aboriginal land rights. This judgement led to the Native Title Legislation and to the establishment of the Native Title Tribunal for hearing Aboriginal claims to land (Lippman 1994).

It is in these historical circumstances and from this resulting situation that Aboriginal literature emanated in Australia. Thousands of years of tradition of storytelling, corroborees and transmission of myths, legends and songs, all provided an impetus to this contemporary literature. Contemporary Aboriginal literature, therefore, occupies a very significant place in Aboriginal history and movement because it is written in the language of the colonisers, adopting new genres and with new purpose and function, in contrast to the literature of the traditional Aboriginal societies, and because elements of the indigenous tradition were preserved and exploited in it. It is, therefore, necessary to appreciate the Aboriginal oral tradition, because that is where Aboriginal literature has its roots and because it provides a background to contemporary Aboriginal literature. As Jackie Huggins rightly observes,

> Aboriginal studies is now concerned with the transformation of an "oral literature" into a written literature, without necessarily destroying the original form in the process. The written mode of expression releases material that was previously to a large extent encapsulated in a local or regional setting, and makes it available for more general distribution and reinterpretation. (1998: 40)

This understanding of the presence of oral literature in the background is important for us here, as oral narration and autobiography are essentially related. To begin with, the Aboriginal oral literary tradition dates back thousands of years. As it was, an oral tradition and secrecy was maintained about the sacred myths, most of it became increasingly inaccessible and gradually disappeared. In recent times some efforts have been made to collect and publish this literature. But since oral narrative became written and Aboriginal languages gave way to English, some inevitable changes may have taken place. Although for the non-Aboriginal reader it may be "merely" Aboriginal oral literature, for Aborigines it is spiritual and totemic as well as historic. It is not mere literature, but, more crucially, culture and history being passed on to future generations. Traditional Aboriginal culture, in fact, does not separate literature from cultural transmission.

Not just their literary tradition but also their languages have either already perished or are perishing. The oral narratives have suffered considerable modifications and loss. Because of such factors, it is very difficult to access Aboriginal literature, except when it is rendered in English. Inevitably, evaluation of this literature has to be on the basis of an understanding of this constraint. So, such Aboriginal oral literature as is available in English becomes the basis for any study of Aboriginal literature for non-Aboriginals. The conclusions we reach from the study of Aboriginal oral literature in English would definitely have been hampered by these factors. On the other hand, it cannot be ignored that white Australians have made a significant contribution to the effort to make Aboriginal oral literature available. However sympathetic they may be their role or presence is bound to have its own mediating effect. For instance, Aborigines may feel consciously or unconsciously constrained to narrate only a particular part of their literature. This may lead to representation of selective memory or other content. On the other hand, it is not impossible that whites themselves may want Aborigines to narrate specific aspects and dimensions and not others or all. All these factors affect our approach to Aboriginal literature, and they must also circumscribe our conclusions from research in this domain.

While we examine the interpretation of the white editor, we may also recall the politics involved in the translation of an oral tale in native languages into written form in English, especially when the coloniser is involved in the translation. Stephen Muecke gives an example of an oral tale transcribed by K. Langloh Parker which goes like this: "Mullian the eaglehawk built himself a home high in a yaraan or white gum-tree. There he lived apart from his tribe, with Moodai the opossum his wife" (1953). Muecke says that this can be contrasted with the work of an Aboriginal narrator Paddy Roe whose English has been transcribed precisely, with pauses indicated by line division:

> Well this fella used to look after the trough he had—
> oh he had childrens too—
> he had childrens—
> he had about five or six children—
> and a old lady—
> mother for the children—
> old man.
>
> (Hergenhan 1988: 32-33)

This example tries to prove how transcription in this instance displaces translation as a strategy for rewriting and the authorship and identity of the Aboriginal narrator are retained thus concentrating more on the linguistic techniques. It also hints at the distortions that are possible in translation.

In this connection, it is relevant to cite some critics who indeed suggest or maintain that such literature of the past has no resemblance to the current Aboriginal situation. Some critics have also questioned the influence of Aboriginal oral literature on contemporary Aboriginal literature. For instance, Mudrooroo quotes Ronald M. and Catherine H. Berndt (*The Speaking Land: Myth and Story in Aboriginal Australia* 1989) who state that the oral literature of the past has little relevance for contemporary Indigenous writers and that the land cannot speak through their work (1997: 23). Aboriginal autobiography, which closely follows the storytelling tradition, also comes in for this criticism. For instance, in his consideration of the "Repressive Hypothesis" Stephen Muecke also says that, with its focus on individual history, autobiography is very far removed from traditional Aboriginal genres; and, having adopted modern western language and genres, they cannot expect to draw on traditional oral literature. This criticism surely seems to have a point at least in theory. But, in contrast, a glance at the bulk of indigenous writings over the last few decades reveals a major, continuing prevalence of interest in the tribal past. This prevalence suggests the importance and the relevance of the past to the current situation of the Aboriginal people. Whatever such criticism may claim, the presence of tradition and orality cannot be ignored.

Let us now look at some oral narratives by way of example. We shall identify some of the crucial issues that such oral narratives manifest. Most available tales embody a kind of warning as to how, if one does not abide by the rules and regulations of the tribe, one will be punished. This aspect provides a clue to one chief purpose of traditional Aboriginal literature. This literature, being part and parcel of Aboriginal life, teaches Aboriginal people how to conduct themselves as members of the tribe. One can consider the effect of such acts of cultural transmission in oral narrative form on the members of a tribe. Similarly transmitted were important cultural values such as respect for nature, kindness to animals, sharing with other living beings and one's roles in a tribe. Aboriginal people believed that their estate had been given to them at the very beginning of time, when the ancestors created the landscape and established the laws and customs which governed family and interfamily relationships (Nyoongah 1994: ix). Aboriginal oral literature seems to embody these customs and laws and pass them on to the future generations as other belongings that are passed on by tradition. Thus, it becomes a record of history, a warning for the future, as well as a set of rules for behaviour in the present.

In his *Introduction to Aboriginal Mythology*, which is sub-titled as *An A-Z spanning the history of the Australian Aboriginal people from the earliest legends to the present day* (1994), Mudrooroo Nyoongah (Mudrooroo Narogin) traces how Aboriginal oral literature is land-centred and reflects that interconnectedness with all of existence, that reciprocity between all, which should not be lost:

> Kinship was and is the tie which binds the communities, not only to each other, but to the stars above and the earth below and the plants, the animals, the very rocks and landscape. . . . The Dreaming is a continuous process of creation which began in the long ago period called the 'Dreamtime'. (1994: vii)

This reasserts how the essence of Aboriginal oral literature is relevant even in contemporary times. Saying that the universe is a biomass, Mudrooroo Nyoongah continues, "we must tend it, for we are the caretakers, and we are not lost souls, but parts of a whole in which everything is related. So we should not pillage and destroy, but co-operate and tolerate, nurture and care for the whole universe with its myriads of living and breathing things" (Nyoongah 1994: xi). No doubt the emphasis is on co-operation, preservation and coexistence. But Aboriginal life was/is not free from conflict. While oral literature depicts the conflict between human beings and nature, contemporary Aboriginal literature represents the conflict between the coloniser and the colonised. Although nature has not played havoc as the colonisers have with Aboriginal life, the conflict that comes through the oral literature functions as a caution to the future generations from the experienced ancestors in a society where age and experience are highly respected and valued. Thus, oral literature sets up a background for the contemporary Aboriginal literature in English. Therefore, our emphasis here is not on establishing a comparison or a contrast between oral literature and contemporary literature, but only on showing how a connecting thread runs through both, although their context, medium, language and situation are different.

Aboriginal oral literature celebrates creation and sings of the harmony between nature and humanity. But it also depicts the tussle between nature and the human being: man trying to subjugate nature and nature trying to subdue or surpass human power. (The tales discussed below, unless otherwise mentioned, are taken from *Wise Women of the Dreamtime: Aboriginal Tales of the Ancestral Powers*, collected by K. Langloh Parker and edited with commentary by Johanna Lambert, 1993.) For instance, the tale "Wahwee and Nerida: The Water Monster and the Water Lily" is basically a love story, but it also explores and exposes Aboriginal beliefs and lifestyle. It portrays a struggle between selfish humans and powerful nature. It tries to establish how possessive and selfish nature also can be, and how, ultimately, human beings are defeated in conflict with nature and must become part of it. It also reiterates the values that Aboriginal women impart to their children, the "nonpossessive and nonacquisitive" values that characterise Aboriginal tradition. Aboriginal children are culturally conditioned from an early age on the principle of sharing. Many available Aboriginal tales establish such an idea or interpretation of tradition.

While many stories depict the conflict between nature and human beings, there are also stories which specifically present women who sacrifice themselves for the sake of their community. Whether the tales come from the belief that women can sacrifice themselves for the sake of the community or from the expectation that they should do so is debatable. Since oral literature functions as a record of the past as well as a code of norms, probably these tales are examples as well as instruction. Although Aboriginal culture and literature proclaim that man and woman are equal, perhaps because of white mediation or intrusion, published Aboriginal tales depict man as warrior and protector and the wiser of the two. And woman tends to be represented as the witch to whom man falls prey. Woman or the body of a young and beautiful woman is compared to a spider in the tale "The Spider." Here an old woman lures men in the form of a young and beautiful woman and kills them. She ultimately turns into a spider after death. Whether philosophical or abstract concepts like youth and beauty, ultimately leading to old age and "ugliness" and bringing about death, are involved in such representations or not, the stereotypical image of woman as an alluring temptress is definitely reinforced here. In the context of the traditional Aboriginal respect for old women and their role in spiritual activities, it is interesting that in this story the old woman disguises herself as a young woman to lure men, as is the depiction of a temptress or a witch.

Johanna Lambert, the editor of *Wise Women of the Dreamtime*, provides a detailed interpretation of each story that is included in this book. She examines the stories taking parallel examples from different contexts, including Hinduism. According to her, "The Spider" contains four levels of understanding, biological, social, psychological and spiritual. Murgah Muggui spins a fantasy of feminine entrancement tempting the victim to discard his marital responsibilities which lead to his unfortunate end. The eight legs of the spider represent the infinite possibilities of feminine or earthly power for change, as well as the four directions and four seasons; "The Spider" reminds us that female spiders of many species devour the male during sexual intercourse. The old woman, apart from representing decay and inevitable death, also reminds us of the role of women in the initiation of men into deep mysteries of death.

As Johanna Lambert says, the old woman represents the mysteries of death, and shows how temptation and denial of duty may lead to death. Since the tales served as instruction, it was an education as well as a code of conduct for Aboriginal men to be strong-willed in order to escape dangers of temptation and to be loyal to one's family and community. The example of a woman, who killed her sexual mates, turning into a spider after death may also have been intended to teach Aboriginal people, especially children, some understanding of nature and behavioural details about various animals and birds. Apart from this, the concept of death and rebirth reminds an Indian reader of the Hindu conception of rebirth on the basis of *karma*, that is to say rebirth depending on the sins of a person in the previous birth. It not only warns men of the dangers but also instructs women how not to be "sexually devouring." This story reminds us, in contrast, of Jackie Huggins' argument in *Sister Girl* (1998) that what Aboriginal women want is the right to say no to white men, unlike white feminists who demand the right to say yes. Here is a woman who attracts men into her web of temptation, whereas the contemporary situation presents Aboriginal women on whom are imposed sexual atrocities by white men.

While we are on the subject of stereotypical images, we may also note that some legends do reinforce positive concepts of womanhood and motherhood. While some of the tales stand witness to the reassertion of the concept of womanhood as caring, protecting and enduring, there are also instances of reinforcing the concept of motherhood in tales like "The Bunbundoolooeys." This tale is about a pigeon that forgets her son and goes in search of food. When she comes back exhausted after a long time and looks for her long lost son, not only does he not recognise her, but he even hurls a stone at her. She dies and her son proceeds with his own life. This story is a clear indication of the responsibilities of a mother, and how a woman may be rejected and punished if she does not fulfill her duties. Mother as a rejuvenating figure is, on the other hand, depicted in stories like "Dinewan the Man Changes into Dinewan the Emu." Apart from voicing society's expectations of a mother, these stories also pronounce the punishment for not living up to them. In a society in which a child is taken care of by the whole community and where the kinship structure provides security for a child, it is interesting to note how motherhood is still considered very responsible. For instance, Ellis and Barwick observe that in traditional Aboriginal society, a woman's success rested specifically on her experience as a mother and full ritual status was available only after the birth of the second child (Brock 1989). This is relevant in the colonised situation of Aboriginal women, who were deprived of motherhood and whose childhood was spent in missionary dormitories and white households as domestics. In the light of the fact that many contemporary Aboriginal texts choose the stolen generation as their subject, this story becomes particularly relevant.

Another striking feature of these tales is the recurrent reference to cannibalism. Against the background of the white assumption that Aboriginal people were cannibals, Aboriginal oral literature's reference to cannibalism becomes significant. It is not of the white assumption alone that we become aware of, but also the Aboriginal assumption of white cannibalism. The tale "The Rain Bird" has Boogoo-doo-ga-da, an old woman with her four hundred dingoes, as the protagonist. She is a cannibal who lures Aborigines with the hope of finding food and then, with the help of her dogs she kills and eats them. One particular sentence raises questions about the context of the story: "she would be sure to meet some black fellows." Does it hint that she is not a black? Is this an oblique reference to white cannibalism? Or can it be that the image of a witch taken from the Aboriginal tales is given a white touch after white invasion? Can it also be a reference to the British queen with her followers, who tempted Aborigines with promises of food and destroyed them? The above questions become more pertinent because these tales were collected and transcribed by white scholars and editors. On the other hand, this story reminds us of "White Lady," who was a famous Koori shaman of the nineteenth century, and whose power was said to emanate from a long red ochre painted staff. On one occasion she is supposed to have made a shamanistic journey to the moon and returned with the tail of what she called a "lunar kangaroo" (Nyoongah 1994: 179-80).

In her interpretation of "The Rain Bird," Johanna Lambert points out that this theme of cannibalism suggests symbolic understanding and utilisation of this practice. The symbolic death and rebirth transform dangerous and antisocial qualities, and the corrupt excesses of Boogoo-doo-ga-da give birth to their opposite, a force of purification that brings cleansing rains. We are reminded of the story "The Spider" for its image of an old woman who lives alone, away from the tribe. While the woman in "The Spider" carries weapons which are forbidden for Aboriginal women, the woman in "The Rain Bird" has a pack of hounds with her which help her in killing people. It is also interesting that the woman in this story turns into a rain bird which predicts rain and which is welcomed and chased away so that it will cry as a sign of rain. It reminds one of the Phoenix which rises out of its own ashes but with a different significance.

Thus, these two stories with strong women protagonists compel the reader to compare them. In a society which perceives spirituality in women and recognises old women as wise on account of their age and experience, the portrayal of women who live on their own as witches, whether they have abandoned the tribe or the tribe has excommunicated them, is interesting. Another striking issue here is man and woman becoming the binaries and man becoming the victim of woman. Aboriginal women were not confined to "four walls" like white women; though they did not venture into the deep forests like men, they did go to gather food with digging sticks and dilly bags. But, surprisingly, the women portrayed in these two stories do not seem to target Aboriginal women. Food and sex being the two temptations in these stories, probably these two stories hint at the dangers hidden in the journey towards two basic necessities of life. For instance, temptation for water is the subject of the story "The Water Monster and the Water Lily." Another crucial issue in these two stories is cannibalism: whether we take the killing of men by women literally or metaphorically, it does bring in the subjects of death and food.

Cannibalism indeed is an important issue in Aboriginal oral literature. For instance, "Eagle-Hawk and the Woodpeckers" (Reed 1998: 64-67) has one man and three women for characters, and all of them are cannibals. The story "The Cat Killer" (*ibid.* 100-3) has Kinie-ger, which has the body and limbs of a man and the head of a cat. He is a voracious eater although no one would have held that against him, for both man and animals must live on flesh as well as vegetable food, says the story. In his introduction to *Aboriginal Stories of Australia* A.W. Reed says that the book may be regarded as a typical sampling of the beliefs of Aboriginals in every part of Australia, which hints that these stories represent the common belief in cannibalism of Aboriginal people across Australia.

As some of the Aboriginal tales themselves raise the issue of cannibalism, white anthropologists and historians also have given different versions of and opinions about instances of cannibalism among Aborigines. Ronaldt and Catherine H. Berndt present the opinions of some of the white anthropologists about cannibalism among Aboriginal people, one of the most debated issues in this field of study. They say, "The Australian Aborigines are not, generally speaking, cannibals who kill other human beings for the specific purpose of eating them. Nevertheless, if the available accounts are to be relied on, burial cannibalism in one form or another is (or was) fairly common" (1992: 467).

Let us also look at some of the other important anthropological and historical studies of cannibalism to which the Berndts refer in their book *The World of the First Australians*. The Berndts say that the Australian Aborigines are not, generally speaking, cannibals who kill people for specific purpose of eating them. They go on to say that burial cannibalism in one form or another was fairly common among Aboriginal people and they bring in the versions of different scholars who have made similar or varying statements about cannibalism among Aborigines. W.E. Roth (1897) discusses burial cannibalism among Aboriginals, the practice of eating select parts of the dead bodies of their own people in different contexts and the argument of A.P. Elkin (1954) also reiterates this. While Lumholtz (1889) and McConnel (1937) also mention cannibalism of corpses, Howitt (1904) reports people being killed and eaten by way of punishment. Howitt draws a distinction between eating one's own dead, "ritual burial cannibalism" and eating the flesh of slain enemies, associated with revenge. Spencer (1914) refers to different practices of cannibalism in tribes like the Mara and Aranda and a number of other tribes from South Arnhem Land, Roper River and north-eastern and central regions. Woods (1879), Basedow (1925) and Bates (1938) suggest infanticide. The Berndts rightly point out that the possibility of cannibalism existed but that many instances may have been exaggerated and embroidered (Berndt and Berndt 1992: 467-70).

Having looked at some of the important issues raised by the available oral literature, let us now proceed to written Aboriginal literature in English. Mudrooroo Narogin rightly observes, "ABORIGINAL LITERATURE BEGINS AS A CRY FROM THE

HEART directed at the white man. It is a cry for justice and for a better deal, a cry for understanding and an asking to be understood" (Narogin 1990: 1). The first complete published Aboriginal work in English appeared in 1929 was David Unaipon's *Native Legends*. Unaipon produced not only sermons and religious treatises but also a vast eclectic body of stories with Aboriginal themes mostly published in mission magazines. He felt that the white man must not leave the aborigine alone and that with a gradual process of introduction of Christianity and all the best of (western) civilisation, the aborigine could come up fully developed (Hergenhan 37). With such statements in the background and his association with the church, one would think that David Unaipon was pro-colonisation and that his book would not have allowed any protest or criticism a voice. But, though the book was only a collection of Aboriginal legends, it was not devoid of political motivation. According to Jody Brown, "Although he [David Unaipon] supported the concept of assimilation, his writing should still be considered political, as it was intended to change white attitudes towards Aboriginal people" (Bird and Haskell 23). Thus, David Unaipon's book paved the way for Aboriginal literature in English with its political overtones. Still, after the publication of this book, it was not until 1964 that another Aboriginal book came out in English, when Oodgeroo Noonuccal published the first book of Aboriginal poetry, *We are Going*.

That the first book of contemporary Aboriginal literature in English was a collection of poetry itself speaks for the significant place that poetry occupies in Aboriginal literature. Adam Shoemaker describes Aboriginal poetry as "poetry of politics." He says, "Verse is not only the most popular genre of Aboriginal creative expression in English; it also clearly illustrates the wide spectrum of Black Australian attitudes to the practice of writing and to the social purpose and utility of literature" (179). Poetry is the most effective and popular genre of Aboriginal literature. Aboriginal poetry is significant for its oneness with the Aboriginal movement and for its rejection of the art for art's sake approach. It embraces the purpose of utility with political significance. What Oodgeroo Noonuccal said in her personal interview with Adam Shoemaker holds a mirror up to the spirit of and expectations from Aboriginal poetry: "I would rather see Aborigines write a book called *Kargun* [Fogarty 1980] than pick up a shotgun" (179).

The Aboriginal storytelling tradition imparts authenticity and spontaneity to Aboriginal poetry in expressing contemporary concerns and situations. In this context, it is necessary to examine the concept of authenticity against the background of Aboriginal consciousness and experience being defined and debated in numerous ways. This is a debate addressed in later chapters of this thesis. It is interesting that the dilemma of writers especially like Sally Morgan raises the question as to how far they can call themselves Aborigines and their experience as Aboriginal experience. For they are urban and urbanised Aboriginal people whose life can hardly be compared without serious qualification with the traditional Aboriginal lifestyle. But, at the same time, it does represent the contemporary Aboriginal experience in different forms. For instance, in Sally Morgan's case it is the experience of an urban, educated Aboriginal woman who grows up with an identity that does not belong to her, as is clearly evident, and who goes in search of the roots of her lineage once she becomes aware of this fundamental discrepancy. In Roberta Sykes' case, it is the experience of a black woman who thinks of herself as an Aboriginal woman and still her people, the community she associates herself with, deny her claim. A look at the identities and associations of Aboriginal women writers presents us with different experiences and situations. Yet it is only fair to say that all of them are facets of Aboriginal experience in a colonised society where native identity is tampered with by the colonisers. This issue will be discussed in the later chapters in some detail. In her article "Commitment and Constraint: Contemporary Koori Writing" Joan Newman discusses Adam Shoemaker's charge (*Black Words White Page*) that David Unaipon's work has a schizophrenic quality. In this context, she argues that Unaipon was writing for a non-indigenous audience and that his generic strategies were designed so as to accommodate these readers. In continuation of this argument, she ironically questions: did he thoroughly contaminate his Aboriginal authenticity? Indeed, she also says that a different question has to be asked here, as to what is authentically Aboriginal for a Koori who uses the printed word in English.

She refers to Mudrooroo Narogin's distinction between Aboriginal writers and writers of Aboriginality, with Aboriginality as a political position (rather than a racial heritage) with continually shifting boundaries. She also refers to the Anthropological school of the 1940s and 1950s which saw the only authentic Aboriginal culture as tribal and traditional and says that the work of these scholars manifests a desire to regard authentic indigenous writers as those who are least influenced by western genre, language use and belief. She goes to the extent of stating that "one of the truths we should now question is the narrow definition of contemporary Koori society as a primarily oral culture, for while indigenous expression is confined to ideas of orality the range of possible avenues of expression will remain limited" (Newman 91). This question of authenticity in Aboriginal literature is related to the larger question of the non-Aboriginal, dominant section of society determining the concept of "Aboriginality" and deciding whether one is "sufficiently" Aboriginal or "not really" Aboriginal. Still, Anne Brewster's argument seems reasonably convincing: "Issues of truth and authenticity, however, don't have to be so daunting. They can be seen as socially specific and politically strategic rather than as epistemologically problematic" (1995: 36).

We can, next, perceive different styles and approaches in Aboriginal poetry as we move from one poet to the next. This poetry expresses both individual and collective grievances and concerns of Aboriginal people in a colonial situation. These grievances extend from early massacres to forced contemporary urbanisation and they bring out the Aboriginal predicament in all its suffering and turmoil. Activism goes hand in hand with Aboriginal literature, and poetry in particular is used as a form of political activism. It works as an outlet for Aboriginal writers' grief, agony and anguish about individual and community predicament. Apart from giving vent to bitter experiences, however, it also celebrates nature and life. It celebrates the time when nature was bounteous and uninterfered with by whites. It celebrates bush life, which was in harmony with nature. For instance, Oodgeroo Noonuccal juxtaposes images like the boomerang and the atomic bomb, and huts and apartments, to emphasise the difference between Aboriginal life and contemporary urbanised life.

It not only brings out the harmony between humans and nature in pre-colonial days but also throws light on the devastating quality of the imposed colonised lifestyle. Although Aboriginal poetry comes up with different individual motives and commitments, in general it agrees with the view that art is not for art's sake, or chiefly a tool for entertainment, but that it should have a function. Aboriginal poetry performs the function of generating awareness among Aboriginal people, of working as the medium of activism of the Aboriginal movement, and of speaking simultaneously to Aboriginal people as well as to whites. This poetry becomes a force in pronouncing the Aboriginal stand on colonisation as well as in the assertion of Aboriginal identity.

After the first collection of Aboriginal poetry *We are Going* by Oodgeroo Noonuccal in 1964, Aboriginal poets started writing and publishing extensively. The 1988 collection of Aboriginal poetry *Inside Black Australia*, edited by Kevin Gilbert, represented almost forty Aboriginal poets. Among the Aboriginal poets whose poetry contributed crucial milestones to Aboriginal literature are, to name only a few, Oodgeroo Noonuccal, Lionel Fogarty, Mudrooroo Narogin, Jack Davis, Kevin Gilbert, Lisa Bellear, Alf Taylor and Anita Heiss. These poets' special contribution can be defined. For instance, Oodgeroo Noonuccal's poetry collections like *We Are Going* (1964), *The Dawn is at Hand* (1966) and *My People* (1970) foreshadow the emancipation of Aborigines, the struggle for citizenship rights and eventually the struggle for land rights. She was at the forefront of all these movements and her poetry grew with them. Apart from the importance of message over aesthetics, Oodgeroo shows a community approach to literature and to poetics. Other Aboriginal writers do not exist in isolation either, but as members of a community. Some, like Lionel Fogarty, use surrealistic techniques to get at the very stuff underlying Aboriginality residing in the condensed and concentrated obsessions of the unconscious, or the individual dreaming.

Aboriginal theatre can especially be perceived as a continuance of traditional oral literature. Borrowing or taking inspiration from corroborees and other rituals, Aboriginal theatre is strongly rooted in Aboriginal literary and cultural tradition. Jack Davis says, for instance, "the Nyoongah language was always full of humour and music. Theatre in a bush arena is the very essence of an Aboriginal corroborree and performances there are often full of brilliant dance and mime. There was and is great opportunity for theatre to draw upon the rich Aboriginal oral literature" (Chesson 197). References to spirits or creation stories and other aspects of traditional culture mark Aboriginal theatre. It blends these with the contemporary situations and themes. Although it borrows from Aboriginal oral literature and has its roots there, Aboriginal theatre is not merely nostalgic, but emerges instead as an authentic contemporary Aboriginal voice. Use of distinctive syntax, vocabulary and words of Aboriginal English are other features that make Aboriginal theatre thoroughly Aboriginal and distinct and different from white Australian theatre. Like other genres of Aboriginal literature, this theatre also is known for its touch of humour, which is a part and parcel of Aboriginal life and literature. As Anne Brewster says, "Humour and laughter often function in this way in Aboriginal culture to parody the systems of authority that have oppressed Aboriginal people. Additionally, humour is a means of coping with the pain and anguish of the past" (1996: 23). Humour works much more effectively and ironically in theatre because of the advantages that the conversational mode of discourse and body language lend to the theatre. For instance, to quote from Jack Davis' play *The Dreamers*,

> Eli: Look at this—busted eye, broken nose, busted eardrum, [pointing to his head] thirteen stitches! You know who done all that? Not *Wetjalas*, but *Nyoongahs*, me own fuckin' people!
>
> Peter: Man, yer wrong, the system done that to yuh, but yuh can't see it.
>
> Roy: How d'yuh expect him to see it, 'es only got one eye, so 'e reckons. (Davis et al 1989: 16)

This touch of humour which lights the colonised Aboriginal world of darkness reminds one of other works such as the autobiography of Glenyse Ward, *Wandering Girl*, where the protagonist thinks that if she had been in the company of her fellow dormitory girls she would have seen only the lighter aspect of the incident and laughed at it.

The first Aboriginal play to be performed was *The Cherry Pickers*, written by Kevin Gilbert in 1968 but published only in 1988. The most important initiative in the evolution of an indigenous theatre was the establishment in Sydney of the Eora Centre for Aboriginal Visual and Performing Arts in 1984 by Robert Merritt. Wesley Enoch, with his production of *Seven Stages of Grieving*, adapted more experimental forms of drama and won widespread critical acclaim. Dramatists like Kevin Gilbert, Jack Davis, Jane Harrison, Eva Johnson, Julie Janson, Bob Maza and others have created and are creating most effective forms of drama, with experiments in theme and technique. Although all of them very powerfully voice the colonised Aboriginal predicament, it is Jane Harrison's *Stolen* (1998) that strikes hardest with its technique and directness. Articulating the agony of the stolen children, *Stolen* gives voice to the vacillations, traumas, turmoils, frustrations, helplessness and rootlessness of the stolen generation which resulted in sexual abuse of Aboriginal women by white men and the phenomenon of unwed Aboriginal mothers.

Aboriginal drama has faced and is facing dilemmas and debates concerning issues such as this regarding its audience: Who is the intended audience? For instance, Jackie Huggins says, "To me that is *My Place*'s greatest weakness—requiring little translation (to a white audience), therefore it reeks of whitewashing in the ultimate sense" (1993: 460). Aboriginal writers have come up with arguments about readership in their writings and discussions, some saying that their writings are for both blacks and whites, some others that Aboriginal literature should not be completely comprehensible to white readers and audiences. Of course, this issue becomes much more important when it comes to Aboriginal theatre, for it is basically written for performance and its success depends on audience participation. Aboriginal drama extensively uses Aboriginal words, connotations and situations, and extensively borrows from traditional Aboriginal culture. For instance, while discussing white audience and Aboriginality in Aboriginal theatre, John Scott says:

> Kevin Gilbert grapples with this dilemma in *The Cherry Pickers*. In a play striving for linguistic credibility, the author is placed in the unenviable situation of elevating the Aboriginal English to make a socio-political point at the expense of the play's naturalism and plausibility (i.e., in the character of Zeena). This problem is increasingly apparent in contemporary black drama, which must strive to make its message clear to both black and white Australians and yet clearly maintain its Aboriginality. (111)

Mudrooroo, in his article "Our World a Stage," also discusses Aboriginal playwrights' attempts to address both black and white audiences by using a combination of Aboriginal English and European theatre convention. He brilliantly analyses the dilemma of an Aboriginal dramatist who has to convey the indigenous predicament and thought but in the western mode when he says, "Indigenous dramatists are schizophrenic in that they must seek to please both non-Indigenous and Indigenous audiences. It is impossible for them to avoid this if they seek to have their works performed in the conventional theatre with its white middle class audience" (1997: 158). This clearly shows that, by and large, the target audience of Aboriginal theatre is not merely blacks but whites as well.

Joan Newman's analysis of the use of Aboriginal English in Aboriginal literature explores a very interesting aspect of the language. She says that the use of various forms of Aboriginal English may limit the readership of even the indigenous readers, for however familiar they are with indigenous idiom in speech they are more likely to be able to read printed texts in standard English than those written in versions of Aboriginal language use especially when dialogue is spelt phonetically (Newman 1996: 83-91). This becomes all the more interesting when read in the light of the argument about post-colonial drama and its strategies in *Post-Colonial Drama: theory, practice and politics* by Helen Gilbert and Joanne Tompkins. This book argues that use of Aboriginal English in Aboriginal theatre forces the "other" to take note of native culture; defines natives by contradicting the coloniser's definition of the colonised; and demands that the non-Indigenous audience put in some effort to understand native culture. In its (at least token) effort to retrieve the lost Aboriginal languages, Aboriginal theatre reminds the indigenous audience and readers themselves of native culture and language. This is also an attempt to evoke awareness of their own (lost) languages among the Aboriginal people.

Loss of language is one of the crucial losses that Aboriginal people have suffered, for it most acutely symbolises loss of identity, culture, oral history and community. Helen Gilbert and Joan Tompkins quote from Jack Davis' play *Barungin* (*Smell the Wind*, 1988) in which an old woman laments that the wetjalas have killed her language. In an attempt to rejuvenate the language killed by the coloniser and to introduce it to the colonising sections as well as unaware colonised sections of Australian society, Aboriginal playwrights extensively use Aboriginal English as well as words from Aboriginal languages. Elsewhere one has seen that a writer like Ngûgî wa Thiong'o may refuse to write in English and start writing in his language Gîkûyû as a mark of resistance towards the coloniser's language and culture. Access to Aboriginal languages is far from easy for today's writers and readers; for most of these languages are quite lost. The only way of recording, remembering and reminding them of these languages through literature seems to be to "nativise" English, especially in Aboriginal theatre. Gilbert and Tompkins make an interesting observation on the use of Aboriginal language in Jack Davis' *The Dreamers*:

> Only those viewers who are fluent in the Nyoongah language will recognise that non-indigenous audience is being constructed as different from the Nyoongah speakers. Similarly, humour frequently functions in precisely this manner since it is the cultural codes of language as much as its specific semantic content that allow some listeners, and not others, to access irony, double entendre, certain nuances, and other potentially ludic meanings. (172)

This example effectively shows how the distanced people distance the distancing people. This use of Aboriginal English functions as a kind of education for non-Indigenous people as well as unaware Indigenous people. Indeed, this issue will assume importance in our study of autobiographies. For just as the playwrights use dramatic devices to educate audiences, the writers of the autobiographies use Aboriginal and western literary devices to achieve the same ends.

While use of Aboriginal English tries to educate both the coloniser and the colonised, what is the message of Jack Davis' plays? What do they argue for? Gerry Turcotte rightly observes,

> Davis' drama does not argue for a return to pre-contact experience. The plays acknowledge the inevitability of interaction, and argue instead for a revitalised understanding of hybridity rather than a reactionary vision of assimilation. This argument for hybridisation—displayed at the level of both theme and form—suggests the potential for Aboriginal culture to enrich and modify white experience, rather than painting the more usual picture of Aboriginal culture being subsumed and ultimately destroyed by the majority culture. (1994: 7-8)

It is a similar kind of hybridity that we come across in the contemporary Aboriginal song, which, in fact, attempts to subvert the colonial forms of art. This is discussed in some detail later with reference to Aboriginal song.

Aboriginal literature explores and is largely based on the historical theme of colonisation and its after effects. The Aboriginal novel, which in most cases is autobiographical, is also concerned with the same subjects. The first Aboriginal novel *Wild Cat Falling* by Mudrooroo Narogin, published in 1965, uses the prison motif. It was followed by his *Long Live Sandawara* in 1979 and Archie Weller's *The Day of the Dog* in 1981. Sam Watson's trilogy, starting with *Kadaitcha Sung* (1990), is remarkable for its experiment with magical realism and for its blend of magic and power, history and horror. John McLaren's *Sweet Water—Stolen Land* (1993) is another remarkable novel. Still, it has to be said that Aboriginal fiction has not yet made as powerful an impact as Aboriginal poetry, autobiography and drama. Similarly, we seem to come across more women writers than men in Aboriginal literature. It is also a fact that women writers mostly write autobiographies and poetry, but not much fiction or drama. And such novels written by women as are available also tend to be autobiographical in nature, like most Aboriginal literature.

Karobran, an autobiographical novel by Monica Clare, is the first published novel by an Aboriginal woman (published posthumously). Two part-Aboriginal children separated from their father are the central characters in this novel, of whom Isabelle is one. The merciless child-welfare authorities are exposed in this novel. It not only depicts Isabelle's untiring search for her father, whom she never finds, but it also seems to assert that black culture survives in spite of all forces counter to it and remains inherently determined in its respect for nature and community consciousness. Another important Aboriginal novel, Faith Bandler's *Wacvie* (1977), is also based on the writer's family history. In her introduction to this novel about her father, she says:

> There were other reasons why the book had to be written. The slave trade of Australia has never been included in school curricula. I have found that most Australians do not believe that slave labour was used to develop the sugar cane industry. Those who were enslaved did not have the opportunity to tell their story. The story has been only told by historians with a detachment from the thought and feelings of the people concerned. . . . All other characters in this book are composites of real people but the main events are true. (n.p.)

A similar concern to tell stories that were not told runs through Aboriginal autobiography as well. One could reasonably extend this concern to all of Aboriginal literature, as to any literature of the marginalised. In this novel about her father Wacvie Mussingkon, Faith Bandler concentrates on the culture, activities, rituals and fears of Aboriginal women who are by and large the major focus of this book. It also looks at the relationship between black female domestics and their white counterparts. This novel, ostensibly about her father, also provides Faith Bandler a context for the presentation of the traumatic situation of Aboriginal women in white colonies.

While the above two novels are family histories, Alexis Wright's *Plains of Promise* (2000) depicts a different dimension of Aboriginal women's life. An educated, urban and self-reliant woman suddenly comes to know about her Aboriginal identity. That becomes the starting point for the dilemmas, traumas and turmoils to which she is then subjected. To her utter amazement and disappointment, she is not completely accepted by Aboriginal people whereas her daughter, who is born of the protagonist's black husband, is. With a blend of supernatural elements and Aboriginal beliefs, this novel succeeds in recreating the contemporary Aboriginal world.

Contemporary Aboriginal literature does not, indeed, appear only in written form. Aboriginal songs also are quite popular as powerful expressions of Aboriginal thought and feeling.[1] Contemporary Aboriginal songs, as live performances and sound and video recordings, relate to the pre-invasion orality of native cultures. The traditional song-man and song-woman are invoked to describe the activities of contemporary songwriters, who are considered the new song-men and song-women. As Beniuk puts it, the contemporary Aboriginal song is both a continuation and a reinvention of traditional Aboriginal culture. It refutes suggestions of cultural stasis and transforms the colonisers' imposed musical culture into a contemporary Aboriginal culture (69-87).

Like their writers of fiction, Aboriginal songwriters too have appropriated and recontexualised white musical genres. They have, of course, also adapted them to black musical forms. Mimicking the forms with which the colonisers are comfortable, they have also introduced an alternative context, that is native oral history, that subverts the legitimisation of colonisation through official versions of history. As Joan Newman rightly observes,

> European writers who publish Aboriginal legends in English are not seen as compromising their European identity. On the contrary, the appropriation of the material of others has been part of their power. Yet the usage of European genres by indigenous writers has rarely been seen as a subversive act, the claiming of a textual space. Rather, it has been interpreted as an indication of the superiority of European models or—more recently—a contamination of the authentically Aboriginal. In either case, the written word continues to be seen as the legitimate inscription of the "West," so that just as the traditional Aboriginal oral narrative may be seen as a bastardised form when encountered in print, so, too, contemporary Aboriginal writing can meet with similar prejudice. (1996: 85)

It is not just by rejuvenating the indigenous music but also by its use in protest against the colonisers and by addition of aspects of white music to Aboriginal music that Aboriginal songs subvert the message of western music. The songs, in fact, have their own purpose. For instance, Yothu Yindi is a political group that sings about the concerns of indigenous Australians. Bob Randall's "Brown Sick Baby," for instance, reads as follows:

> Between her sobs I heard her say,
> "Police bin take-im my baby away.
> From white man boss that baby I have,
> Why he let them take baby away?
> Yaaawee, Yaahaawawee,
> My brown skin baby they take 'im away." (Beniuk 73-74)

This song most poignantly reflects the predicament of the Aborigines. The Aboriginal movement and literature have been constantly concerned with the issue that this song raises. This song, in brief, says that Aboriginal women had children from white men, mostly their "bosses"; that children born to Aboriginal women and white men were taken away and the white bosses/fathers did not object to this. The "brown skinned baby" opens the whole discussion of the issue of half-castes as well as predominance of considerations of colour and the threat to part-Aboriginal children. These songs, thus, emphasise the issues that dominate Aboriginal literature written in English.

Aboriginal songwriters Kev Carmody and Archie Roach have both appropriated the "male singer/ songwriter 'genre'" (Beniuk 74) which has emerged in contemporary western music. It represents both a deconstruction of the notion of "good singing" and a construction of the singer/songwriter's "authenticity." Even as they appropriate this "genre," Carmody and Roach draw upon their contemporary Aboriginal discourses and their post-colonial Aboriginal meta-texts. They seem to combine strategically the genre of the singer/songwriter with the Aboriginal tradition of the song man to produce contemporary Aboriginal songs. Aboriginal beliefs about death, burial and nature are referred to by way of criticism of colonisation. Carmody has also been active in print, writing of "Illusions such as Equality, Democracy and Capitalism and Christianity" and calling for a separate Aboriginal nation. He proclaims, "Our own financial system, flag, laws, language and education system could be implemented and Black Australians could be accepted as a nation of communities" (Carmody 4). Ruby Hunter is one of the Aboriginal women singers and songwriters who is supposed to have contributed to a fundamental change in views regarding women in the thinking of the Australian music industry. David Beniuk argues, "theory, or no theory, we can see in the practice of contemporary Aboriginal song generally a struggle to find spaces for contemporary voices to generate a continuity and a method of achieving this is through the continuation of oral traditions" (87).

According to Beniuk, "the performance of these traditional songs is recontextualised by their placement on, for instance, a Western stage or a compact disc. They therefore represent a textual hybridity, a response to colonisation as well as the continuation of a tradition" (86). Mudrooroo recognises formation of a hybrid music that may be seen as Australian as well as Indigenous. But he also attacks the postcolonial academics who have coined the term hybridity to refer to such things as contemporary Indigenous culture. He states that defining culture as pure or hybrid seems to be a trap into which postcolonialists have fallen (Mudrooroo 1997: 108). Helen Gilbert and Joanne Tompkins rightly observe:

> Indigenous song/music recalls pre-contact methods of communication, affirms the continued validity of oral traditions, and helps to break the bonds of conventional (western) representation. As part of a slightly different strategy, hybrid song/music often function to protect the domination of the coloniser's linguistic/musical tradition by liberally interspersing it with the words, forms, or music structures of a less well-recognised and validated system of communication. (194)

In his prologue to *Australian Literature: An Historical Introduction* (1989) John McLaren says: "The history of Literature in Australia is a story of how writers struggled against the alienation, by denying it, by learning to accept it and by attempting to transcend it" (McLaren xix). Against this background, it is also necessary to look at women's writing in Australia, as the present study specifically deals with Australian Aboriginal women's writing, where gender also plays an important role. Kay Schaffer, in her book *Women and the Bush* (1988), says that the Australian tradition is blind to women and that the Australian national identity is related to the masculinisation of a national culture. Miriam Dixson, in her *The Real Matilda: Woman and Identity in Australia 1788 to the Present* (1976), states that there is a profound unconscious contempt for women which pervades the Australian ethos. She elaborates this view by saying that Australia has a literary tradition which produces a profound sense of sexual loneliness and an awkwardness or fear about the flesh of women. In *Damned Whores and God's Police* (1975), Anne Summers analyses the position of women in Australian society as a colonised sex.

We can thus see that women writers have started questioning the very concepts of womanhood and wifehood that concern both mainstream and Aboriginal societies. In the same way, the stereotypical glorification of childhood gets dismantled in Australian women's writing. Indeed, it is almost an essential part of these works for very good reasons: a girl child's world of loneliness, frustration and abuse, for instance, is exposed and explored in these writings as a particularly significant subject in the light of colonial history of treatment of children. This applies more to autobiographies of women. This may occur in a mainstream writer as well. For instance, Christina Stead's *The Man Who Loved Children* (1940) unveils the traumatic childhood and adolescence of a girl who struggles to free herself from the domestic turmoils and gender abuse. Childhood is an important aspect of Aboriginal women's writing and their lives for reasons beyond a white girl child's experience. Aboriginal childhood, especially for a girl child, is all the more traumatic as we have seen in the reference to dormitory existence and the stolen children scenario. Such special factors of all significant stages of Aboriginal women's life will be discussed in detail in the later chapters. Coming back to white women writers, writers like Henry Handell Richardson (Ethel Florence Lindsay Richardson), known for her novels like the trilogy *The Fortunes of Richard Mahony* (1930), Eleanor Dark who made a mark with her novel *The Timeless Land* (1941) and Christina Stead, whose novels like *Man Who Loved Children* (1940), *For Love Alone* (1944) and

The Little Hotel (1973) have contributed tremendously to women's writing in Australia, and have tackled themes of enormous significance which characterise Australian history, culture and ideologies as well as the lives and visions of women. Novelists like Jean Bedford, Janine Burke, Han Mckemmish, Kate Grenville and Barbara Hanrahan reveal real concern with the female voice and they tell hitherto untold stories—readings of social legends, of history, or simply of individual experience.

Apart from white writers like Patrick White, Xavier Herbert and Les A. Murray who dealt with Aboriginal issues and Aboriginal characters in their own way, there are also white women writers whose themes were centred round Aboriginal issues and characters. Novels like Nene Gare's *The Fringe Dwellers* (1961) and Thea Astley's *A Kindness Cup* (1974) carry on the tradition of Catherine Susanna Prichard whose novel *Coonardoo: the well in the shadow* (1929) had dealt with Aboriginal exploitation. Although men have published works with Aboriginal issues at the centre, women's works had linked black and female oppression, perceived similarities in the oppression experienced by blacks and had dealt with the devastating oppression of black women. Glen Tamasetti and Nene Gare's works aim to delineate the history of women and to draw out more clearly the forgotten struggles of women's lives. Mary Durack's *Keep Him My Country* (1955) is another novel which deals with Aboriginal issues.

It is true that white writers, especially women writers, have, indeed, dealt with Aboriginal themes and characters. But their treatment of these issues has always been limited, if not also controversial. One of the major allegations against such writing is that Aboriginal people have remained stereotypes in it. It is believed that it fails to explore the pathetic tales of Aboriginal massacres and has been written from a white coloniser's perspective. Hence, Aborigines, specifically Aboriginal women, resist identification with the national type. Most Aboriginal societies are supposed to be matriarchal societies and every family has a strong mother figure, unlike the white societies. This contributes to a lot of difference between the concerns and problems of Aboriginal women and white women. For instance, in her article "Aboriginal women, politics and land"

Peggy Brock says, "Unlike western societies, where gender has been a marker of empowerment (male) and subordination (female), gender in Aboriginal societies defines different fields of influence and empowerment. This gender-specific authority is protected by maintaining a separation between male and female spheres" (2001: 9). White women writers may have written about Aboriginal women. But one wonders if they identified themselves with Aboriginal women at all. We must also wonder whether Aboriginal women accept the portrayal of their characters in white women's writing. Do they identify themselves with white women? Can some of the issues that the white feminists consider or analyse concern Aboriginal women at all? Do Aboriginal women accept these as their issues? How much has the bias of gender contributed or failed to contribute to colonisation, subjugation and discrimination? It seems, also, in part, that Aboriginal women write in protest against the image of Black women in white writings. In Jackie Huggins' words,

> It is also apparent that Aboriginal women are viewed as the "other" based on a menial or sexual image: as more sensual but less cerebral, more interesting perhaps but less intellectual, more passive but less critical, more emotional but less analytical, more exotic but less articulate, more withdrawn but less direct, more cultured but less stimulating, more oppressed but less political. (1998: 36)

Some of these issues will be discussed in the second chapter of the present study titled "Protest as Watchword."

Against this brief historical background, we may now be able to look at the following issues and the questions emanating from them: What was the condition of Aboriginal women before 1788, the advent of the British in Australia? What are the sources for any study of this question and how reliable are they? What caused a change from traditional status to the contemporary predicament and image of Aboriginal women? What is the present status of Aboriginal women in Aboriginal society and in white Australian society? Is there an awakening among Aboriginal women inspired by white culture about their condition in their own Aboriginal societies? Has the condition of Aboriginal women improved or worsened after

1788? Why and how? Particular questions about Aboriginal women's writing come next.

For instance, what is the purpose of Aboriginal women in writing for publication—to propagate their ideas, to express their fears and problems, to awaken society, to revolt against existing literary or social norms? When we read the autobiographies chosen for the focus of the present book, it becomes clear that their consciousness emanates from the authors' being women, black women, Aborigines and being exploited and oppressed. But which of these factors influence the writers most and dominate or mould their writings? What is the role of Aboriginal culture in the construction or composition of Aboriginal women's image and their autobiographies? How far do they fairly or usefully project matriarchal Aboriginal society, the culture of the bush, Aboriginal art and music, the conventional Aboriginal images of Aboriginal women and two hundred years of servitude on the fringes of white society?

An attempt is made in the present book to explore and discuss the above issues and questions. But there are some serious limitations to a study of this kind. For instance, my being an outsider to Australian and Aboriginal Australian society and the difficulty in obtaining both published and archival material. Lack of sufficient secondary or critical material may also limit to an extent the analysis of the works examined. The general questions on Aboriginal women's autobiographies raised by others as well as by the present study have included the following: Why does this research project focus on Aboriginal women's autobiographies? It is always interesting to study the voices of women and the marginalised sections of any society, for they have been silenced violently or otherwise effectively for ages in most cultures; their oral composition and writings echo their cries of agony and voice their otherwise silent protest. When it is women belonging to the marginalised sections, more violence may be used to silence them, and a double burden of oppression is thrust on them. Hence their cries are much more heartrending. This is one of the reasons why my research is centred around the self of Aboriginal woman as it is expressed in her autobiography. And my being an Indian, a woman and a witness to innumerable cases of exploitation and subjugation of disadvantaged groups on the basis of race, caste, class, colour, religion, region and gender, and infinite number of movements against this treatment in the past and in the present which may extend into the future—these are factors in which some sort of identification is possible. There is, however, another reason particularly worth mentioning here—that even when oppressed men's writing has drawn much attention, as yet oppressed women's writing seems to have received very little attention.

The next basic question concerns the choice of autobiographies. It is a fact that most Aboriginal literature, like any other marginalised literature in its beginning, is autobiographical. Any work of Aboriginal literature may have done for a study of the expression of the self. But what interested me particularly in women's autobiographies was, how and how far this self that is expressed informs an overt claim to expression? When the veil of fiction is lifted from autobiography, what shape does this expression take? How much of the self does it express? How "auto" are these autobiographies? How much of the narrative relates the experience, and how much of it is expression of reaction to the experience? How much of this response is intellectual and how much emotional? If it is the experience of the writer at some point of her life that is being voiced, is there no difference between her self then and her self at the time of writing? And which of these selves do these autobiographies deal with? How appropriate is it to call such narratives autobiographies? How does one deal with their "authenticity" with the play of "selective memory"? How do we discover the silences in an autobiography and judge their role or function in the narrative? For instance, in her autobiographical novel *Karobran* (1978), Monica Clare leaves out some of the crucial details of her life such as her first marriage, her divorce, and separation of her child by legal action. There is no doubt that this is an important link in her life. Why do we suddenly see the young girl Isabelle become a mature woman? Against the background of such questions, it is quite obvious that one cannot obtain from one study a "complete" picture of the self or life in an autobiography. But in spite of these limitations, the form of autobiography does succeed in giving the scope to the writer to express her "self" that is denied to fiction or fictionalised accounts of a life.

Although the emphasis of this study is not so much on the genre, let us take a bird's eye view of the theoretical context in which Aboriginal women's autobiographies may be situated. This, in no way, is an ambitious effort to summarise or quote the whole lot of discussions and arguments on autobiography that have so far been published. Autobiography is an area which is much explored and debated. But, there are still some to be discussed and explored. Various developments and movements in different fields have either added to the already existing debates on autobiographies or questioned them. Autobiography, which tries to express, represent, define and discuss one's own self, has been widely experimented with in form, content, style and subject. Let us look at some of the immediately relevant theories of autobiography.

James Moffett's (1968) observation that autobiography usually involves the writer looking back through a distance of time that permits him to disengage his present self from his former self and to understand now what he did not understand then, surely has substance and merit. He goes on to say that thus, the story is about growth and self-knowledge. No doubt Aboriginal women's autobiographies look back at the former self but in this attempt, they look at the society, state and their community as well. Self-knowledge is coupled with community knowledge. Aboriginal women writers have also experimented with the form of autobiography. Content becomes, in some cases, more important than form. They also tend to alternate from form to form—chronicles, reports, diaries and autobiographies according to the context and need, though it is difficult at times to identify the exact difference between these. Sometimes all these forms occur in the same text. This modification or transformation of conventional form gives rise to several interesting points worth discussing. These are discussed in detail in the chapter of this study titled "Protest as Watchword." Moving between forms, facts, experience and interpretation, these autobiographies create a new world, refusing to fit into the frame of western theory and practice.

As Cockshut (1984) rightly observes, it is only when the question of point of view becomes crucial for the reader that an awareness of autobiography as a separate form emerges. It is exactly this point of view which is crucial in Australian Aboriginal women's autobiographies, which voice the concerns of the writers who are subjected to multiple subjugation on the basis of race, class and gender. It is in this context that Anne Brewster's view of Aboriginal women's autobiographies as "autobiographical narratives" rather than "autobiographies" comes in. She admits that though she has settled for the term "autobiographical," she recognises that these texts examine the author's own life within the context of those of other family members and that these texts are both autobiographical and biographical (1996).

James Olney, who has made a significant contribution to an understanding of autobiography, says, "They seem different things, study of the self and study of the world, yet the two cannot be ultimately separated, as subject and object join and merge in consciousness" (1972: 14). This statement is an appropriate description of the blend of individual and community in these autobiographies. It is true that, as the genre suggests, they are, chiefly, or most obviously, means for expression of the self. But that is not, certainly, all. It is not liberation of the self alone but an effort towards the liberation of the race as well that forms an objective for individual writers in an identifiably oppressed society. All experience becomes one and one's experience represents all experience. These writers hail from different social, political and economic backgrounds, but they have one thing in common, their Aboriginality—their culture, their past and present and the big question about the future. Inheriting rich Aboriginal culture and suffocating in a discriminatory society, their common concerns naturally are with the loss of the past, suffering in the present and the threat in the future to their identity.

It will be all the more interesting to note the opinion of a critic who looks at the genre from a gender perspective. According to Estelle Jelinck (1980), women's autobiographies differ from those of male writers in form and content and that they tend to emphasise the personal much more than the public. Australian Aboriginal women's autobiographies prove that they are different from men's autobiographies. But the difference is not so much about being personal and ignoring the public. For, most of the time these writers use "we" or even if they speak as "I," it reaches the readers as "we" by implication. A majority of these writers emphasise the political aspect of Aboriginal life and describe their involvement in the Aboriginal movement. Although private life is not completely missing from these books, it seems the writers' community consciousness makes them give significant attention to the collective experience.

In their effort to be faithful and goal-oriented, Aboriginal women's autobiographies remind us of "testimonio" (Beverley 91-114), in which the narrator represents a social class or a group and speaks for or in the name of a community or a group. This gives voice to a previously "voiceless," anonymous, collective popular democratic subject, the people. As Aboriginals, as women and most importantly, as Aboriginal women, these writers come out and address their people as well as the oppressing section of the society. These autobiographies, therefore, carry a representational value and basically perform a representational function. There may be several Aboriginal communities and hundreds of dialects in Australia. But their autobiographies in English represent the struggle of a displaced people and culture at a general level as well.

We may also think here of "autoethnographies" (Lionnett 1989), a form in which writers' interest and focus are not so much the retrieval of a repressed dimension of the personal self, but the rewriting of their ethnic history, the re-creation of a collective identity through the performance of language. Like Bernice Johnson Reagon's "cultural autobiography" (1982), Aboriginal women's autobiographies become locations to keep crucial and culturally specific memories to reclaim a history and construct a community of strength and diversity. The fundamental questions about autobiography that Doris Sommer raises in her article "'Not Just a Personal Story': Women's *Testimonios* and the Plural Self" are particularly relevant to these autobiographies:

> Is [autobiography] the model for imperialising the consciousness of colonised peoples, replacing their collective potential for resistance with a cult of individuality and even loneliness? Or is it a medium of resistance and counterdiscourse, the legitimate space for producing that excess which throws doubt on the coherence and power of an exclusive historiography? (Brodzki and Schenck 111)

The autobiographies selected for study express nostalgia for the past, the period prior to the colonisation, that colonisation against which they naturally, perhaps even inevitably, protest. This nostalgia helps them in their lament over the loss of indigenous culture and also becomes one of the devices of postcolonial protests that echo against imperialism, if not always attempting glorification of native culture. As postcolonial autobiographies,[2] they reflect the writer's responsibility and desire to change the genre as well as the relations of power in society. Not only nostalgia but also a sharp focus on the conspiracy of silence over the predicament of women in Aboriginal societies, contributes to the emphasis on the sufferings of women in Australian society. Usually, this happens indirectly. A sense of loss about traditional Aboriginal societies that permeates Aboriginal women's autobiographies succeeds also in pronouncing the notion that everything about Aboriginal societies is bright, green, plentiful and cheerful. Thus these autobiographies operate as a forum for the writers to argue their case against injustice, deprivation and humiliation, even as they reassess their past and present culture. Jackie Huggins rightly articulates in *Sister Girl*, "I believe writing was so important to me because it was a liberating experience. Issues of race. class and gender began to appear much clearer" (1998: 108).

Mudrooroo Narogin claims that autobiographical narratives fix history in a static sense rather than fluidly ranging towards future concerns. He goes to the extent of calling them "death books" (1990). And he adds that he finds writing fiction more liberating because it allows the writer to go forward rather than backward. But he also admits that the account of a life or autobiography has a place in traditional Aboriginal literature and so the genre is not completely a western importation. Thus, Mudrooroo Narogin appears uncertain in his assessment, especially about using the genre as a political weapon. Aboriginal women have adapted autobiography to use it as a weapon against, among other things, racial discrimination and political subjugation. If the same kind of criticism is used against his own autobiographical novels, Mudrooroo Narogin's own novels can be dismissed on the basis of his adapting not one but two western genres, novel and autobiography, and for being self-obsessed throughout. If autobiographies are death books, his autobiographical books are also death books, although perhaps with some difference. Yet the major difference between Aboriginal women's autobiographies and the autobiographical novels of male writers like Mudrooroo Narogin is that women writers refuse to make self-obsession either the central theme or the chief objective of their works. They do not write just about their selves but also about the community and about their selves as members of that community. In her article "Race, Gender and Identity: *My Place* as Autobiography," Joan Newman says that *My Place* is primarily concerned with the meanings of selfhood in terms of relationships, particularly those of family, and even more particularly those that can be traced through the matriarchal line. She says,

> The depiction of selfhood in relational terms, emphasising one's interdependence with others, is considered to be a characteristic of women's autobiography, rarely to be found in works written by men. It may also be interpreted as a characteristic of Aboriginal autobiography in which the idea of joint ownership of a narrative is a more common understanding than ideas of single, originating authorship. (Bird and Haskell 71)

In a way, Anne Brewster also reiterates this opinion while discussing *Don't Take Your Love to Town*. She rightly points out that the genre of autobiography is gendered and the specificity of this female experience means that the narrative is different from the male tradition of autobiography. Brewster quotes Susan Stanford Friedman's article on "Women's Autobiographical Selves" in which the writer argues that where men's autobiographies construct a notion of the solitary and privileged individual, women's autobiographies invoke not so much personal and individual histories as collective cultural histories (1996: 37). That way the women writers, taking liberty with genres and structures, achieve, if not an ideal, at least a significantly different purpose, and perhaps in this respect their works are more powerful (or differently significant and useful) as political weapons than the works of men.

These autobiographies may be seen as chapters in a collective memory of common experience. For example, among the writers,

Rita Huggins and her brothers and sisters were removed from their parents and placed in the dormitory on Barambah Reserve. Ella Simon, Ruby Langford, Della Walker, Evelyn Crawford and Eileen Morgan in New South Wales were not separated from their kin by the dormitory system; and yet they were confined to reserves and missions; Mabel Edmund and her parents worked on cattle stations. The assimilation policy made different kinds of impact on these women's lives, although eventually they all, almost invariably, became domestic servants working for middle-class white men and women (Moreton-Robinson 10).

Most Aboriginal writers are, themselves, mixed blood children—a fact that symbolises the Aboriginal situation. To be specific, most of them are dormitory children. The "Stolen Generation," which was exposed to western education so as to be converted into "good" domestics and "good" Christians, has significantly used that minimal education to express itself and to recollect and retell its untold stories. That most Aboriginal writers of today belong to the stolen generation is an important historical and political fact. This is one of the themes that recurrently appears in Aboriginal literature and shapes the personal narratives and influences the tone of the writers. Most of the texts discussed in this book, for instance, were written by writers who were urbanised, educated, self-reliant and actively involved in the Aboriginal movement, with a background of removal from Aboriginal societies and the care of parents, and of dormitory life and domestic servanthood. As Jack Davis rightly puts it, in his interview with Adam Shoemaker "The Real Australian Story," the stories in Australia have "all been told. But a lot haven't been told enough—and quite a lot haven't been told *properly*. Everything's been said but I think there's a lot we still have to learn" (Turcotte 1994: 47).

The second chapter of this book, titled "Protest as Watchword," examines how this protest shapes Aboriginal women's autobiographies. This protest against racial discrimination, and incidents and accidents consequent to this, is voiced sometimes directly and sometimes subtly and indirectly, sometimes consciously and sometimes unconsciously. In any case, it is true that basically these autobiographies function as vehicles to convey the writers' vehement protest and resistance. How they attempt to deconstruct the history and Aboriginal identity created by the whites and to reconstruct the history and Aboriginal identity forms the main argument of the chapter, apart from a glance at the subtle ways in which they are conveyed.

The third chapter titled "Multiple Voices of the Writer" presents the writers as women, Aborigines and Aboriginal women. Although, of course, it is not easy to differentiate between these voices, it is not impossible to identify them either as they reach the readers sometimes separately and sometimes simultaneously in these autobiographies. Concerns and interests may shift and the tone may change from work to work but the Aboriginal woman's consciousness never ceases to dominate all these autobiographies. This fact leads to the recognition that these writers inhabit spontaneous multiple identities.

The fourth chapter titled "Conflicting Identities" deals with these multiple identities and shifting priorities and viewpoints. Apart from their identities as Aborigines, women and Aboriginal women, the writers we study also have other identities (or facets) depending on their colour, religion, region, background and individual qualities and capabilities. These differences or identities raise conflict, within the writer, between the text and the self, and the self of the writer and the readers/critics. How this conflict gives rise to important questions about the whole Aboriginal issue and Aboriginal literature will be examined in this chapter.

It would not be out of place to mention here that while we deal with several autobiographies, some of them may be analysed at length and in detail, and others may not. This does not at all mean that some are given prominence and others not or that some are more important than others. The difference arises from the controversies that the texts have raised and the attention they have received. On account of the white interference in some texts, the length of the book, the specific features of the genre, the particular issues that are raised and the concerns of the writer, some texts may be more frequently quoted and discussed.

The concluding chapter will make an effort to draw parallels with some of the issues that are raised about identity in Aboriginal men's autobiographies. It will also try to suggest parallels with and raise similar issues and concerns that become the preoccupation of Indian Dalit and Tribal literatures. Rather than drawing parallels in every chapter with Indian Dalit literature, comparative suggestions will be confined to the concluding chapter and there will be suggestions or possibilities for future study.

The autobiographies that form the primary sources for the present book are: Margaret Tucker's *If Everyone Cared* (1971), Ella Simon's *Through My Eyes* (1978), Monica Clare's *Karobran: The Story of an Aboriginal Girl* (1978), Shirley Smith's *Mum Shirl: An Autobiography* (1981), Elsie Roughsey's *An Aboriginal Mother Tells of the Old and the New* (1984), Sally Morgan's *My Place* (1987), Ida West's *Pride against Prejudice: Reminiscences of a Tasmanian Aborigine* (1987), Glenyse Ward's *Wandering Girl* (1988) and *Unna You Fullas* (1991), Ruby Langford Ginibi's *Don't Take Your Love to Town* (1988), *Real Deadly* (1992) and *My Bundjalung People* (1994), Marnie Kennedy's *Born a Half Caste* (1990), Alice Nannup's *When the Pelican Laughed* (1992), Mabel Edmund's *No Regrets* (1992), Evelyn Crawford's *Over My Tracks: A Remarkable Life* (1993), Rita Huggins and Jackie Huggins' *Auntie Rita* (1996), Roberta Sykes' *Snake Dreaming* (3 vols. 1997, 1998, 2000), and Ruth Hegarty's *Is That You Ruthie?* (1999).

NOTES

1. My argument on contemporary Aboriginal song has been obtained from and greatly influenced by David Beniuk's article "Contemporary Aboriginal Song in a Postcolonial Context." *nlr*, 31, Summer 1995, 69-87.
2. The term "postcolonial" in the context of Australian Aboriginal literature is discussed in detail in the chapter titled "Conflicting Identities."

Protest as Watchword

Two centuries of mute suffering and discrimination explode in Aboriginal literature and provide a key to the element of protest in Aboriginal women's autobiographies. If literature is the battlefield of Aboriginal women writers, protest is their weapon and resistance their strategy. These writers narrate the inhuman treatment meted out to them, but going by the autobiographies studied, never with a touch of self-pity. These autobiographies reflect their sense of anger, anguish and protest. They do not embody an acceptance of their predicament but an endeavour towards change. Literature and activism go hand in hand in expressing Aboriginal resistance to subjugation and assertion of Aboriginality. This chapter will examine how this protest against discrimination and exploitation is voiced in the choice of genre, language, theme and technique of these autobiographies.

Being the moulding factor of Aboriginal women's autobiographies, protest comes out through subverting the images created by whites and in writing alternate histories. This seems to be an effort to alter every description or category or label that has been created and nourished with a colonialist attitude. In altering these images and writings, Aboriginal women writers adopt different strategies. They speak in the colonisers' language but speak against them, adopt colonisers' literary tradition but subvert it, adopt the colonisers' strategy but attack the colonisers themselves. In doing so, these writers do not imitate the colonisers but innovate strategies of resistance against them.

One of the major complaints of Aboriginal literature against whites is that history has always been written from the colonisers' perspective and that the exploiter has written about the exploited and their experience without referring to the exploitation. Thus Aboriginal women's autobiographies try to fill the vacuum created by white history as far as the Aboriginal version of history and the Aboriginal voices in history are concerned. In the process, these autobiographies become alternate histories instead of remaining personal records of experiences and feelings of individuals. In presenting their personal life or portraying their family history, consciously or unconsciously, these writers deconstruct the history written or assumed by the settlers and reconstruct their native history. Anne Brewster rightly observes:

> By reclaiming and rewriting history Aboriginal women intend educating both black and white Australians. For white Australians this education has the purpose of revealing the violence of colonisation which has been suppressed in official histories. For Aboriginal people the narration of the past has the additional role of producing a sense of unity and group solidarity. The awareness of a common past can thus bind together people who have been dispossessed. (1996: 53-54)

The common past that Anne Brewster refers to seems to be the binding factor in Aboriginal women's writing. Aboriginal women seem to express collective experience from collective memory to create a collective consciousness. Even when these writers use "I," it sounds like "we." Most of the time these writers use "we" in autobiographies which are supposed and expected to be individual. The story of the self becomes a story of the community with a purpose to rewrite and recreate the community history. Lack of their own version of history motivates these writers to create alternate histories in the form of autobiographies. For instance, in her autobiography *Is That You Ruthie?* Ruth Hegarty says that her story becomes the story of her fellow dormitory girls and her experiences and feelings reflect their experiences and feelings as dormitory girls. Aboriginal women writers hail from different economic and political conditions. But, they have their culture in common as well as their past, present and a great uncertainty about their future. Their common concern for the loss of their Aboriginal past, the suffering in the present and the threatening future unites them.

Sally Morgan, in her *My Place*, expresses her agony over absence of history written by Aboriginal people:

> Well, there's almost nothing written from a personal point of view about Aboriginal people. All our history is about the white man. No one knows what it was like for us. A lot of our history has been lost, people have been too frightened to say anything. There's a lot of our history we can't even get at, Arthur. There are all sorts of files about Aboriginals that go way back, and the government won't release them. . . . I just want to try to tell a little bit of the other side of the story. (163-64)

Sally Morgan not only expresses her agony over the brutalities and atrocities of whites against Aboriginal people but she also demands that those records or that part of the history should be made generally public or at least be accessible to the Aboriginal people. That these files are maintained not by the National Library but by the police itself reveals that the records were kept not as part of an effort to preserve history but only as secret records. Sally Morgan's overt statement that expresses her desire to write the other side of history is not confined to her and her autobiography alone but becomes a very crucial issue for most Aboriginal women writers and their autobiographies as well.

A "half-caste" Tasmanian Ida West repeatedly narrates her and her people's attempts in her childhood to achieve assimilation into white society and repeated rejection by mainstream Australian society. She also represents the heart-rending tales of the half-castes by citing her personal experience. The contempt of the whites for the natives comes out in its true form in the episode in which West's house is set on fire by a white who adds abuse and curse to the already horrendous atrocity. Ida West not only presents her own version of the stories of her times but also tries to take the help of other sources to construct the history of Aboriginal people under colonial rule. She refers, for instance, to a letter written by a Hobart Town white gentleman as early as 1819, published in the *Asiatic Journal of Calcutta*, India, in the following year, which expresses concern over the racial discrimination in Australia. She quotes:

> Several interviews have lately taken place between the people of the settlement and the Natives of the west coast; who, as appears very probable, are debarred from all intercourse and interchange of sentiment with their countrymen on the eastern side, by that lofty

> range of mountains which intersects the island from the northern to the southern extremity. From the fearless and unsuspicious deportment of the former in these interviews, it would seem that the hostile disposition of the latter towards the people of the settlement was rather provoked by bad treatment than the spontaneous effect of their native ferocity. (West 105)

Such records, which should form a crucial part of history, are unfortunately missing from white versions. This is only an example to show how Aboriginal writers try to reconstruct history not only through their personal experiences and autobiographical writings but also by citing "historical evidences" in order to achieve their purpose. This reconstruction of history does not only deconstruct the history written by the other but also vehemently condemns certain incidents that have reinforced discrimination against Aborigines. To quote Anne Brewster once again, "Aboriginal memory preserves the unwritten black history of colonisation, which has been emerging in the public arena in the form of life stories of Aboriginal women. Aboriginal memory is transforming public perceptions of the past in post-invasion Australia" (1996: 6).

Whether it is Sally Morgan who writes with a desire to tell the other side of the story or Ida West who writes with a consciousness that all these days only whites had been writing about the Aboriginal people, or whether it is Rita Huggins who maintains that her book is a record for her children and grandchildren and will speak to other people including whites about the story from the Aboriginal side, or Ruth Hegarty who says that whatever she writes would reflect the feelings and experiences of her fellow dormitory girls, or Elsie Roughsey who demands that the world should know what was not mentioned or Ruby Langford who dedicates her *Don't Take Your Love to Town* to every black woman who's battled to raise a family—they are all part of rewriting and reconstructing of history by each writer in her own way. For instance, in her *Sister Girl,* Jackie Huggins says,

> I wanted to write about the silent history of Aboriginal women that has been the experience of so many of my mother and grandmother's generation. Although we learnt about the pioneering ef-

> forts of mostly European males, little was recorded about the "backbone" of the pastoral industry, the Aboriginal men and women who toiled as stockmen and domestic servants. This is so much a part of Australian history and it is about my history. The stories deserve recognition and need to be rescued, recorded and shared. (1998: 1)

Not only is white history subjected to deconstruction and subversion in Aboriginal women's narratives, but also is the image of the Aborigines constructed by whites. They try to counter, overtly and covertly, the image of the Aboriginal people that whites have been depicting as ugly, uncouth, aggressive, cruel, ignorant and many other qualities associated with the colour black. The accounts of Aboriginal life in Aboriginal women's writing reconstruct the image of Aborigines as subjugated and suppressed and also project them as a race with spiritual strength that has survived and will survive in spite of the eliminating and exploitative policies once followed and are still being followed by the colonising race. In doing so, they assert and reassert their Aboriginal identity. But, this assertion of Aboriginal identity is juxtaposed as a direct counter to the hiding of their Aboriginal identity by previous generations. Thus the writers unveil how Aboriginal people were effaced or how they were forced to acquire false identities since they were scared of being subjected to humiliation, harassment and of the threat of removal of their children from them.

For instance, Sally Morgan's *My Place* depicts three women belonging to three generations, grandmother, mother and daughter. The grandmother tries to hide the Aboriginal identity of her family, in fact she seems to be preoccupied with the threat of her family's Aboriginal identity being recognised. This makes the family live under the disguised identity of Indians. This is balanced by Sally Morgan later who proclaims her Aboriginal identity and starts on her search for her place and her roots. Her revelation of the fact that her grandmother was scared of disclosing her Aboriginal identity and was scared of the police, unfolds a hitherto untold tale of deprivation and misery. This change in Aboriginal women over generations that is evident in the responses of Sally Morgan and her grandmother towards racial discrimination is not an example of the changing policies of the white government but of the changing attitude of Aboriginal people. That they have come together and are ready to fight against the white policies is revealed in their assertion of Aboriginal identity.

Assertion of Aboriginal identity being the main focus of Aboriginal autobiographies, descriptions of Aboriginal beliefs, culture and lifestyle help to give it substance, to make it more emphatic. They supply the missing link in Aboriginal history. Native belief in spirits, foreboding, bird calling, initiation and other practices are repeatedly referred to in these autobiographies. Not just a mention of them but the writers' belief in the same is also established. This implicit criticism seems to aim at the imposed western religion and the apprehension that it may clearly be, even when not asserted, a move toward building native beliefs once again. It does not necessarily mean that these writers do not believe in Christianity, for many of them are Christian by religion. I shall discuss further in my fourth chapter, "Conflicting Identities," the assertion of identity by Aboriginal writers, the identity crisis that they go through due to their split identities, which are created by the way they are perceived by white society, Aboriginal society and Aboriginal women writers themselves.

These autobiographies give vent to the writers' nostalgia for Aboriginal culture. All of them lament over the loss of important features of indigenous culture like corroborees, community life, association with nature and spiritual approach to life and the world. This expression of loss of culture and spirituality strengthens their incessant battle against segregation. Detailed descriptions of hunting, food gathering and cooking are some of the means of expressing their nostalgia. They rejoice in describing such details and assuring themselves about the community's belief in supernatural elements. For instance, in *Pride against Prejudice*, Ida West describes how effective indigenous medicine is: "We made our own soap out of dripping and we used mutton-bird oil for rubbing our chests for flu. Garlic in your shoes was a remedy for whooping cough. We could boil the buzzies from the vine of the bush and bottle" (40). Belief in spirits is another characteristic feature of Aboriginal life which finds a prominent place in Aboriginal women's writing. Ruby Langford Ginibi, for example, reveals, "I knew the house was full of spirits. When we were kids we used to hear the gate click shut, and footsteps on the veranda and down the hall. We weren't frightened, it was our home and they looked after us" (1988: 63). Ida West and Sally Morgan also discuss how they have always felt the presence of the supernatural. Sally Morgan describes how a bird predicted her grandmother's death. Great reverence and concern for preservation of nature are also predominant in these autobiographies. White Australian literature depicts the conflict between man and nature, man's relentless efforts to subjugate it and his eventual defeat at its hands. But Aboriginal literature celebrates nature and sings of the harmony between human and nature. Direct attacks on racial discrimination and reiterated references to Aboriginal culture mould these autobiographies as the voice of a whole culture's longing for freedom from discrimination and exploitation. This explicit and implicit protest against white supremacy is successfully conveyed in these autobiographies and makes them especially valuable as personal as well as vivid cultural and political documents.

* * * * *

Since Aboriginal women writers basically protest against colonisation and discrimination, they attack policies of the white government, specifically those policies that affect the Aboriginal people drastically in the name of welfare. Hence, these autobiographies protest not only against white-constructed Aboriginal history and identity but also against the manipulations of the government. It is ironical that the natives of Australia were "given" citizenship rights only in 1967. Ironically, this sanction of citizenship rights inflicted more restrictions on the Aborigines, increased the interference of the government in Aboriginal issues and legalised some of the atrocities against them, for instance, removing the "half-caste" children from Aboriginal societies and parents. As it was discussed in the introductory chapter, these children, mostly half-caste children, were removed on the pretext that Aboriginal people were not capable of looking after their children or that these mixed blood children could be civilised. Removing them from their parents and putting them in dormitories and civilising them was the responsibility of the government and missions. Some of the children were removed in the name of education too. The sanction of citizenship recognised the hitherto non-existent Aborigines but they had to face more complicated problems now. Indeed, Aboriginal writers call citizenship rights "dog license" to express their contempt and anger towards the white concept of their citizenship rights. Ruby Langford Ginibi, in her autobiography *Don't Take Your Love to Town*, goes a step further and vehemently criticises the Aborigines Protection Board also:

> Those days, you hardly saw Kooris in pubs, because liquor was prohibited. People who did go to pubs had to show a Dog Licence ("Citizen's Rights") and if a white person was caught supplying liquor to blacks he was given six months without the option of a fine. Aboriginals were all right to join the services and fight for the country that we had no say in, but you couldn't breast a bar with your mates for a beer. The Dog Licence was a product of the Aborigines' Protection Board. And now I understood why Dad was so against the idea of the Board funding me to go to teachers' college The main function of the Aborigines' Protection Board was to discriminate against Aborigines. (1988: 48)

What Ruby Langford Ginibi says about the Board is echoed in other Aboriginal autobiographies as well. The single paragraph quoted above brings in so many issues for discussion and echoes protest of so many: the fact that Aboriginal people have no say in their own country; Aboriginal participation in the war on behalf of the white Australian government; Citizenship Rights given to Aborigines by the white government are almost universally attacked. The Aborigines Protection Board and its unjust and atrocious interference in Aboriginal lives in the name of welfare is laid bare. It also brings out the fact that whites were prohibited from associating themselves with Aborigines. Ginibi's reference to her father's distrust of the Board also unveils how Aboriginal people were not inclined towards the welfare boards created by the white government.

Aboriginal women writers express their protest against the government policies that adversely institutionalised the Aborigines. As Ruth Hegarty says in *Is That You Ruthie?*: Aboriginal people were institutionalised for reasons known only to the government. Her words, "never daring to," mould her autobiography and decide to express not only her dormitory experiences, but also those of many others like her. These are not mere words but the condition of Aboriginal life. This was the situation not only of Ruth Hegarty. From other Aboriginal autobiographies too we gather that this was the predicament of most Aboriginal people, and this is the inspiration behind Aboriginal literature, and in particular, Aboriginal women's autobiographies. "Never daring to" is the phrase that silences Glenyse Ward, this is the condition that Monica Clare portrays, this is the situation that conditions Ella Simon, this is the predicament that was inflicted on Margaret Tucker, and this is the fear that haunts Sally Morgan's mother and grandmother, to mention only a few.

Is That You Ruthie reveals how fear ruled the life of Aborigines and how their life was institutionalised and how this institutionalisation was intended to produce stereotypes. Ruth Hegarty says,

> my story is their story; whatever I write would reflect the experiences and feelings of all. Our lives were governed by the same policies and what happened to one, happened to all of us. No one was treated as special or given special privileges. We were treated identically, dressed identically, our hair cut identically. (4)

The common suffering leads to collective identity and community feeling. It develops a sense of sisterhood among the girls. But the equality that Ruth Hegarty refers to is not an equality with the whites, not an equality with all other human beings, but only an equality among the institutionalised Aborigines. Her words stand witness to the fact that "identical" was the word that decided the perverse fate of the dormitory girls. Does this identical appearance ironically lead to protest against the shared predicament of the colonised? Is equality used as a means to suppress individuality and eliminate liberty? This equality, this identical appearance only helped in producing stereotypes deprived of individuality and independence. Not only was their future decided but also their liberty was curtailed, expression silenced and actions constrained. Ruth Hegarty narrates her childhood that was imprisoned, silenced, constrained, insecure and stressful.

Not just individuality, but "privacy" was another word that was unheard and unfound in the dormitory. Nor was it just lack of privacy but was also humiliation, especially as girls, that was inflicted upon them. The dormitory girls, even the older ones, had to undress before the authorities before going to bed. Ruth Hegarty recollects, "Taking off every stitch of clothing including bloomers, we put on a white calico nightie and, before walking up the stairs, we still had to lift our nighties in the light of a torch or a lantern to reveal that we had nothing on underneath" (58). The humiliation of the dormitory girls did not end there but it extended into the classroom and even took the form of sexual abuse. Ruth Hegarty even witnesses some of the girls abused by white male teachers. This awareness led dormitory girls to excessive cautiousness. They were silent but cautious enough to fold their arms tight and make sure that the blouses were pinned right up to the neck. As Aboriginal dormitory girls they were subjected to tension, nervousness, and to an experience of walking on a razor's edge of perverse regulations at a tender age, with nobody around to comfort and console them. Their identity crisis also haunts them early in life, for adulthood was thrust on them. They vacillated between being a girl child and an adult. Like everything else this identity of girlhood was also inflicted on them, which increased their insecurity even as the indignities of womanhood were simultaneously inflicted on them. Ruth Hegarty recollects her bewilderment as a four and a half year old child upon being told that she is a grown up girl now and that she cannot stay with her mother any longer: "That morning I was my mum's baby, that afternoon I was a big girl. I was expected to take responsibility for my actions" (Hegarty 27).

These autobiographies protest against the dual imprisonment of the Aboriginal people in the name of mission homes in childhood and in the name of Aboriginal identity in adulthood. They protest against deprivation—deprivation of home, of parental love, care, community life and liberty. Elsie Roughsey Labumore, in her *An Aboriginal Mother Tells of the Old and the New,* reveals that the home that made them dormitory girls in the name of protection was not "home" at all: "Too much work, also too many belting, but it was all dormitory customs. There was no sympathy at all for us by anyone. They, who were in charge of us, were rough and cruel" (15). Ironically, they were removed in the name of protection, but they had no protection there and they were exposed to loneliness, starvation, displacement, inhuman treatment, humiliation and sexual abuse.

Ruth Hegarty says that her book would tell the hurt and pain that the girls suffered of being separated from mothers and families. It has to be remembered that most of these girls in the dormitory had single parents. This again is the consequence of the colonisation, which resulted in divisions like "half-caste," "quarter-caste" and "part-Aboriginal." Because of the white blood in them, whites thought, they were more educable and hence could get rapidly assimilated into white society. Whether assimilation into white society happened or not, they were certainly alienated from their culture and their people. They were deprived of community life, love and warmth of parents, care and protection of their own people and were trained to become good domestics.

* * * * *

Aboriginal literature regularly expresses anger and frustration and this anger and frustration lead to contempt for the English, the language of the colonisers, which too is reflected in Aboriginal literature. Oodgeroo Noonuccal, an inspiring force behind the Aboriginal movement as well as literature, says that English is a bastardized language and that Aboriginal people use English not out of love for it but because that is the only medium available to them to communicate with other Aborigines and whites, given the fact of the elimination of Aboriginal languages. Roberta Sykes, another Aboriginal writer, also reiterates the fact that Aborigines in reserves were forced to adopt English. On the other hand, they exploit their enemy's language strategically to protest against the enemy. The major criticism frequently levelled against these writers is that they fight against western imperialism and yet they adopt the same western language and literary tradition. Yet English had become the only link language in a situation where hundreds of Aboriginal tribes existed with innumerable dialects; indeed many Aboriginal languages are even mutually incomprehensible. Then what about literature and forms of literature? Is it appropriate for them to use the western tradition of autobiography, for instance, given the assumption that autobiography is a western tradition? This is one of the questions posed by critics. Leaving aside the presumed rigidities of literary tradition and racial assumptions, when one has to communicate with another, one must ensure that the listener understands the speaker's voice. And if that means using a commonly understood yet colonially inherited language or genre, so be it.

Not only against language but also against literary forms do the Aboriginal women writers wage a war in their autobiographies. Sally Morgan flouts the rigidities of form by making her autobiography itself raise the controversy as to whether it is an autobiographical novel, or an autobiography or a biography. The life stories of her mother, grandmother, and her grandmother's brother also become part of her own autobiography. Rita Huggins' *Auntie Rita* is a narration by Rita Huggins and a commentary by her daughter Jackie Huggins is a crucial part in it. Ida West's autobiography is more like a chronicle with newspaper reports, dates and many other details. Oodgeroo Noonuccal's autobiographical fiction *Stradbroke Dreamtime* is an experiment with the conventional genre. Her childhood experiences become short stories for children in her autobiography. The first part of it deals with these and the second part deals with Aboriginal legends. *When the Pelican Laughed* and *Mum Shirl* were originally narrated, not written, and documented by others. *Karobran* by Monica Clare presents the writer's own experiences but in a fictional mode. All these works are considered as different forms of autobiography that writers have experimented with. *Auntie Rita* which is neither a biography nor an autobiography in a strict sense is also taken into consideration. Similarly, personal narratives recorded and transcribed by others, for instance *When the Pelican Laughed* by Alice Nannup, are also included in the present study. This is only to make a point that for Aboriginal women writers, what mattered was their purpose of writing their life regardless of definitive choice of genre. The present study considers autobiography in its extended, often inclusive, sense and hence works like *Karobran* find a place in our discussion.

All these writers have admitted that they have no particular fascination for the genre of autobiography, and like any literature of the marginalised, Australian Aboriginal literature also starts with personal narratives, gradually widening its scope. For instance, Roberta Sykes says, "It is not something that I chose. I would write entertaining novels. Not a choice. I, like all the black writers, have the social goal to educate and liberate the community and that is the first criterion" (Personal Interview 9 January 1998). Thus her preference for the genre is decided by her responsibility towards the race. It is not the writer in her but the activist in her who chooses the genre in which she writes. Ruby Langford Ginibi asserts in her autobiography that one "dreamline" is more powerful than an autobiography. But since everyone cannot understand the significance of dreamlines, she has to communicate by means of her autobiography. Although Aboriginal women adopt the form, they do move away from the tradition of autobiography in its strict sense. What is important for them is the expression of Aboriginal feelings and thoughts; they owe their allegiance to these and not to the narrative tradition. Contents take the primary place and push the form to the secondary place. One may contrive the form but new life is infused into it by this practice. Even the language they use is full of culture-specific Aboriginal words, deeply embedded in Aboriginal life and consciousness. These autobiographies prove that literary rigidities and theories cannot stand, cannot withstand the vehemence of protest. These writers succeed in achieving their aim of spreading awareness and sharing experience through their autobiographies. As postcolonial autobiographies, they throw light on the writers' responsibility and both the necessity and their own ability to change the genre as well as the power relations in society. It is not their allegiance to the genre but their belief that their life stories rather than fiction is the more effective medium to reach the readers. This is the inspiration behind the writing of Aboriginal women's autobiographies.

These experiments with the genre of autobiography raise innumerable questions in the reader's mind. Why do they make this attempt to experiment with genre? Is this a mere experiment for experiment's sake? If it is an experiment, what did the writers want to experiment with, the genre, voices in the autobiography or the writer's liberty? If it is not a mere experiment or, at least in some cases, not a deliberate experiment at all, what was the purpose behind writing an autobiography without strictly adhering to the genre? Australia seems to have a very strong tradition of autobiography, starting from the personal narratives of the early settlement times. Is that the reason why Aboriginal women writers chose or had to choose autobiography? Did they think that this is the only genre in which they can express themselves? Even if it was not a deliberate attempt of the writers to adopt autobiography, and they found it easier to adopt from their tradition of story telling, is it not a fact that the writers gave more importance to the contents and not to the form and that the so-called western tradition of autobiography served the purpose of Aboriginal people to unravel the mysteries and atrocities of colonialism?

Trying to rewrite community history and common experience, and to write autobiography, which reflects a very personal experience—how could these come together and achieve the effect that the writers wanted to achieve? How does one's experience become the community experience and one's lifetime experiences represent more than two hundred years of colonised experience? Aboriginal women writers do not provide any clear or direct answers to these questions, except by way of a few statements about the genre of autobiography. Instead, it is their work that provides clues and answers to the above questions.

Aboriginal writers have also had to face criticism that not only did they depart from the native tradition by adopting a western tradition but also by turning their autobiographies into a complaint against society, for Aboriginal literature by tradition is a celebration of existence and nature. When asked about this criticism, Roberta Sykes, for instance, poses a counter question: what is there to celebrate in colonised Australia? (Personal Interview 9 January 1998). It is one of the great achievements of Aboriginal women writers that they have not only moulded forms and narrative techniques of western literature but also the tradition of native literature to suit their contemporary and immediately relevant needs.

* * * * *

Aboriginal women writers, though very conscious about women's issues, do not identify themselves with white feminists or associate themselves with white feminist movement. In fact, they try to distance themselves from the white feminist consciousness about women's issues. Jackie Huggins rightly observes in her powerful book on Aboriginal women, *Sister Girl*,

> Despite the predominance of patriarchal rule in Australian society, Australia was colonised on a racially imperialistic base and not on a sexually imperialistic base . . .white racial imperialist ideology granted all white women, however victimised by sexist oppression, the right to assume the role of oppressor in relation to Black men and Black women. (1998: 14)

As an Aboriginal woman, Jackie Huggins tends to identify herself more with Aboriginal people of both genders than with white women. This throws light on the Aboriginal contention that it was race that played havoc with them and it was their racial identity that was played with most. This view strengthens the consciousness of an Aboriginal woman that is all-pervading in most Aboriginal women's writing—whether it is Sally Morgan or Ruby Langford Ginibi or Ruth Hegarty or Elsie Roughsey Labumore or any others. This also raises the issue of the participation of white women in the exploitation and colonisation of Aboriginal people. The sisterhood that Jackie Huggins defines and establishes is the sisterhood among Aboriginal women and not the sisterhood between Aboriginal women and white women.

Jackie Huggins not only dissociates herself as an Aboriginal woman from white feminism but also vehemently attacks it. She says:

> Black women feel no sense of relief to find that they are dealing with a white woman instead of a white man in these matters. Many say they prefer to deal with white men because they then escape the missionary-style zeal that some feminists employ in their belief that because they are feminists they are experts on *all* and that Aboriginal women need "raising up" to their level of feminist consciousness. And so we see that colonialism is alive and well in the women's movement. Some feminists behave just like the mission-

> aries' wives who wanted to raise Aboriginal women to the lofty heights of white women's sex roles and Christianity, too arrogant to realise that Aboriginal women's traditional social, political and spiritual roles gave them a far better position than white women could ever imagine. (1998: 31)

This is not prioritising white man over white woman, but only trying to prove how white women are different from and are indifferent to Aboriginal women. Huggins seems to be emphasising the fact that Aboriginal people, especially Aboriginal women, have faced equally bad treatment from white women, whose power is due to their race but not due to their gender. Interestingly, Jackie Huggins seems to suggest that there was not much of a difference between the Christian missions spreading Christianity in order to "reform" Aboriginal people and the white feminists' attempts at spreading awareness among Aboriginal women in order to "reform" them. The assertion of Aboriginal identity, specifically Aboriginal woman's identity in the form of a protest against white feminism is expressed by saying that Aboriginal women are in a much better position compared to white women and that the concept of white feminism does not really suit them or is not really required by Aboriginal women. In doing so, Huggins does not segregate white women but protests against the segregations created and maintained by white feminists as whites and as white feminists. Gender gets eliminated when Jackie Huggins discusses the whites who colonised and exploited the Aboriginal people, since it was their racial identity that dominated when they colonised and subjugated Aboriginal people. That the white women writers were mostly silent about the sexual abuse of Aboriginal women by white men, except for a few feeble and unconvincing voices like Catherine Susanna Prichard, may have triggered indignation in Jackie Huggins against white feminists. She states that unfortunately white women think that they own feminism and that it is a false proposition.

Aileen Moreton-Robinson refers to the Indigenous Medical services which used Depo Provera in the 1970s as a cheap contraceptive and how it did not work properly and led to spontaneous abortions in Aboriginal women. She reveals that Depo Provera was banned in the United States in the 1960s and it was not approved as a contraceptive in Australia, yet indigenous women were experimented upon. Moreton-Robinson says, "Whereas feminists demand legal abortions, Indigenous women want stricter controls over abortions and sterilisations because they have been practised on our bodies without our consent" (171). Aboriginal women became guinea pigs for the experiments conducted by the white government just as they also became a dumping ground for banned medicines. It is also important to recall the background of Aboriginal women not having any rights over their children, who were actually "stolen" from them by the government. Whereas it is a question of liberty and sexuality for the white woman, it is a question of race, motherhood, and liberty in a community context for the Aboriginal woman. Hence Aboriginal women cannot identify themselves with white women, whether they are feminists or not. It is not Aboriginal women who create segregating boundaries, but it is the discriminating white society and the racist white government which have already created these differences.

Jackie Huggins' observations provide a detailed and thought-provoking introduction to this issue: "Today, while many white women have won their fight to get out of their kitchens, Black women are still fighting to get in, but this time tailored to their own specifications" (1998: 23). White women's activities, she feels, have to be seen as part of colonisation and oppression of Black women. Sisterhood is not powerful enough to transcend such racial boundaries. Once again, Jackie Huggins brilliantly analyses the difference between white women and black women and indigenous women's reluctance to join white women's liberation movement:

> The white women's movement was at that time concerned with sexuality and the right to say "yes," to be sexually active without condemnation. For Aboriginal women, who were fighting denigratory sexual stereotypes and exploitation by white men, the issue was more often the right to say "no." Where white women's demands to control their fertility were related to contraception and abortion, Aboriginal women were subject to unwanted sterilisation and continued to struggle against the loss of their children to interventionist welfare agencies. While Aboriginal women insisted on their right to have access to full medical services, including infor-

> mation about contraception, their demands to control their own fertility were related to the right to have as many children as they wanted. (1998: 27)

This statement is not only a criticism of white women's attitude but is self-explanatory since it puts the Aboriginal woman's plight and fight in a nutshell. The liberty to say no to the white man, the liberty to have as many children as possible and keep them with her—are the concerns of the Aboriginal woman, whereas the white woman's concerns are the opposite. For white feminists, gender discrimination comes first and for Aboriginal women racial discrimination stands first.

The picture so far drawn in this chapter will remain inadequate in representing Aboriginal women writers, for it is not only the resistance against racial discrimination but also against gender discrimination that informs their work. Although majority of these writers concentrate on white atrocities against black women, there are writers like Ruby Langford Ginibi who move across the boundaries of race in order to look at the gender conflict within their own race. It is true that in her autobiography, sensibility and concerns of a woman dominate her Aboriginal consciousness. She takes her love to town repeatedly and fails miserably. She is exploited by one man after another. Unable to come out from the longing for familial relations and feeling insecure about her children, she proposes companionship or accepts companionship of men repeatedly. Ultimately, with the failure of every relationship, she remains alone with her children. With all these vagaries of life and her tasks to be achieved, she becomes increasingly sensitive to women's problems. She not only strongly condemns, for instance, her own daughter being beaten up by her son-in-law but does something about it, too:

> He said something but I didn't give him time to answer. I belted him and knocked him over the lounge and flattened him.
>
> "I didn't raise my daughter to be bashed and kicked by bastards like you." I threw him out. I don't know where I got the strength from. (Ginibi 1988: 206)

The position of women in Aboriginal societies, at least going by the implicit reports in Aboriginal women's work, was secure and equal to that of men. But in the mainstream society, an Aboriginal woman's life becomes twice miserable as a woman and as an Aboriginal woman. Ruby Langford Ginibi points this out when she says,

> I felt like I was living tribal but with no tribe around me, no close-knit family. The food-gathering, the laws and songs were broken up, and my generation at this time wandered around as if we were tribal but in fact living worse than the poorest of poor whites, and in the case of women living hard because it seemed like the men loved you for a while and then more kids came along and the men drank and gambled and disappeared. One day they'd had enough and they just didn't come back. (1988: 96)

Although her Aboriginal identity remains with her, it acquires derogatory meanings and ghastly consequences in a colonised society. She is deprived of community life, sense of security and sense of belonging. She remains a nomadic tribal wandering all over in search of work and shelter and carrying the responsibility of her children. Although she is a "tribal" because of her identity, consciousness and life style, she fails to get the security that tribal life provides. She does not seem to suggest that Aboriginal societies are ideal, but definitely proclaims that the position of a poor Aboriginal woman in Aboriginal societies is safer and more secure compared to that of her position in an urban white society. Not just insecurity, but also poverty haunts her and as a poor Aboriginal, single mother, with no stable shelter and work, Ginibi raises her voice against the hardships that are inflicted on women like her. The breaking up of families, especially Aboriginal families, moves her to tears since she not only identifies with the situation but is also reminded of her mother's "elopement." These are the long suppressed shrieks of a woman in a displaced cultural atmosphere. The women are rooted out from their own tribal atmosphere and they have to live in the city alienated from it. They are always reminded that they are tribals and hence segregated from society. And yet there is no security and tranquillity of tribal society.

Even though Aboriginal women writers represent discrimination and exploitation among Aborigines themselves, again it turns out to be a criticism of the colonisers. These writers believe and de-clare that this discrimination and exploitation among Aborigines is due to the influence of the settlers and their cultural assimilation with white society. Such a criticism of their changing value system is another aspect of these writers' work that strikes hard at the "mainstream" culture. The rapidly increasing crime rate among Aborigines, for instance, could be seen as a revolt arising out of frustration caused by subservience and insult. Sometimes Aboriginal identity itself becomes the reason for being accused of crimes not committed. Aboriginal women writers expose many such burning issues. In doing so, they not only attempt to trace the roots of these issues but also try to address them through their literature and activism.

Activism constitutes a major aspect of the writers' concern for social, cultural and political issues. In some of the autobiographies discussed in the present book, especially Shirley Smith's *Mum Shirl* and Ruby Langford Ginibi's *Don't Take Your Love to Town*, we come across a major turn in the writers' lives as they become associated with overt movements against harassment and discrimination by whites. These autobiographies, apart from coming to us as literary experiments in form and style, also contribute to the records of personal life and history that provide an inspiration for other Aborigines and become eye-openers for the whites and other readers elsewhere. For instance the life story of Mum Shirl. Shirley Smith, fondly addressed as Mum Shirl, is one of the fourteen children born to Aboriginal parents living on a mission in New South Wales. From the time she first went to visit her brother in jail, she started visiting other prisoners as well. And she stood by people in trouble, whether in jail or outside, people without homes, people without families and those who have lost hope. She worked for Aboriginal Medical Services and in the 1970s she was particularly active in the Land Rights Movement. She became the guardian for people who were troubled by the white law.

The story of Ruby Langford Ginibi, a mother of seven children, is different, yet as powerful and relevant. She strives hard to carry the yoke of family responsibilities. In the process she loses some of her children. In the later part of her life when her grown up children are subjected to harassment, her scope broadens and her concern shifts gradually from the particular to the general. She starts working in the direction of emancipation and betterment of the lot of Aborigines. Thus her struggle goes on, and slowly takes the shape of struggle for the survival of the whole race:

> I started noticing articles about black deaths in custody. There were ten Aboriginal prisoners for every one white prisoner. Many more black men died in prison than whites, and there were often suspicious circumstances—an inquiry that was held in the cell by one (white) man and was over in thirty-five minutes, and so on. There had been no real inquiries.
>
> I knew quite a lot about what went on inside prisons. Nob, David, Steve, James, Patrick and Horse all had stories to tell, though they kept most of it to themselves. I knew that. But I knew Nob had been bashed by police, that tear gas was used on riots, that there was not adequate counselling for prisoners, that prison broke people's spirits, and it was killing our sons like a war. (Ginibi 1988: 224)

Like the previous quotation from Ruby Langford Ginibi, the words quoted above also sum up the police atrocities on Aborigines. This heart-rending predicament of Aborigines contributes to such a complete change in the perspective of Ruby Langford Ginibi that she turns her attention from her own children to the suffering of the race. Oodgeroo Noonuccal's words hold a mirror to the Aboriginal movement and the Aboriginal spirit for activism in her interview, "Recording the Cries of the People," with Gerry Turcotte: "this old clichéd business of saying we are non-political. If you're non-political, man, you're dead, you're not even thinking. So this was another 'fear' thing that they put into the unenlightened to keep them from rocking the boat" (Rutherford 19).

* * * * *

Deborah Bird Rose examines two dimensions of silence in connection with Aboriginal literature: silence as an active voice and as a passive condition. She says that active silence is a characteristic of the indigenous system of knowledge, as well as of a religious and political life. She quotes from MacKinnon:

> Passive silence derives from the deployment of power to stifle or destroy people and their knowledge. This form of silence is thus characteristic of regimes of terror . . . and is a principal tool in colonisation. As is well known, colonisation depends on erasure. . . . Where silence previously existed as an active voice, the practices that stifle and ultimately erase thus work a double damage: not only suppressing people's audible voices, but reconfiguring the meaning of their silences as well. (MacKinnon 1987 in Brock 92)

We come across both active and passive silence in Aboriginal women's writing. Colonisation conditions the life of the colonised and the life of the dormitory girls gets more conditioned, for their identity as colonised, orphaned, Aboriginal dormitory girls contributes to the conditioning of their lives at different levels. Silence becomes very eloquent as it conditions the voices of Aboriginal women and speaks about the intentions and repercussions of the silence, one form of which is destructive and the other constructive. Silence becomes more eloquent than eloquence in that it throws light not only on the indigenous culture, resistance to colonialism, protest against discrimination and attachment to Aboriginal identity but also on colonialism, discriminatory policies and exploitation of Aboriginal people, especially Aboriginal women.

The two forms of silence, that is, one inflicted by whites and the other adopted by indigenous people, are in a way interconnected and also connected with the policies of colonisation. Because the silence inflicted on Aborigines is oppressive, Aboriginal writers decide to withhold information and adopt partial silence, and the silence inflicted and the silence adopted are both related to the colonised-coloniser relationship. The silence that is inflicted on the Aborigines has only one function, to silence the Aboriginal people. But the silence that Aboriginal people adopt has two dimensions, that is the conditioned silence and the powerful silence that is actually the power to withhold information. The second type of silence is used as a very strong weapon of protest by Aboriginal writers. The reluctance to speak about certain issues is juxtaposed with the assertion that the exploited should talk about the exploitation and only Aboriginal people should write Aboriginal history. Thus, there is a longing to voice condemnation of whatever has been written about them and also a deliberate silence in Aboriginal women's writing. Whether it is conditioned silence or deliberate silence, silence in Aboriginal women's writing is even more eloquent than words; it says more than what has been said in words. This silence raises many questions, reflects the psychological conflict of the writer, throws light on the conditioning forces, provides a clue to the indigenous thought system and gives a silent voice to the powerful protest.

Let us first examine how silence throws light on the conditioning or how the writers depict the silence that pervaded their childhood dormitory life. The most heart-rending narration that comes before the readers is that of Ruth Hegarty in her autobiography, *Is That You Ruthie?* It is silence that becomes the code of conduct in her dormitory life. It is silence that rules every minute of her life and it becomes a barrier not only for her expression but also for her communication with her mother who stays on the other side of the wall. Hegarty says, "We ate our food in complete silence. There was no way I could call out, 'Good morning, Mum, how are you this morning?' Neither could she call out to me. Already I was learning how best to conduct myself as a dormitory girl without getting into trouble" (28-29). Her conditioning in the home as a dormitory girl depends on its inflicting silence on her. It is this silence that makes her repress her feelings, it is this silence that makes her lose her individuality and fit into the role of a good dormitory girl and it is this silence that takes away from her the power and inclination to question. As a child she was deprived of the most comforting and relieving expressions of trouble, crying. As motherless children, dormitory girls were not even allowed to lament on the loss. They were hushed up and humiliated for doing so, "I kept most of my feelings to myself. I wasn't able to show any sort of emotion, we were not allowed to cry. . . . Crying always resulted in punishment" (30).

In silence, loneliness, oppression, "identical treatment," loss and suffering, childhood turns out miserable for the dormitory girls and silence becomes a further burden on this misery. At least there is a streak of sarcasm in Ruth Hegarty's words, but a writer like Glenyse Ward in her *Wandering Girl* confesses that as dormitory girls they were taught not to speak unless they were spoken to and even if they were spoken to, to speak the minimum. But this silence is not devoid of protest. In fact this is a silent protest. Ward naively walks into a party though as a black servant she was ordered by her mistress not to come out before the guests. Although this seems to be a naïve act on the surface, it definitely is a very powerful silent protest. This protest does not stop here, but silently works against the oppressive white mistress. Afraid of going into the garden to pluck lemons for her mistress's juice, Glenyse Ward uses the stored lemons against orders. Again, against orders of the mistress, Ward eats from the expensive and refined cutlery in her mistresses's absence. When she flies away into the world of freedom from such restrictions and domestic servanthood, she does it silently.

Ruth Hegarty reveals in her autobiography that she silently wrote to her mother, instead of requesting her mistress, about the need to hike her salary; her mother wrote to the superintendent and he wrote to Hegarty's mistress. She raids the grapevine to which she was not allowed any access by her mistress. She comes before the guests without the white starched cap and apron she is required to wear for these occasions. Thus silence becomes a strategy of protest and protest becomes the outcome of silence and the essence of silence. Thus silence speaks volumes about the turmoil that goes on in the mind of the writer, about the need to adopt silence and how it bursts out in the form of action. This is Aboriginal women's resistance against silence, oppression, exploitation and discrimination that they are subjected to. And this is also resistance, in the language of silence that they are made to learn from the system. Thus not only do they express resistance in the colonisers' language but also turn the strategies that are used against them to express their resistance. And thus they give silence and overt subversion a voice that is more audible and more effective than any other language.

Silence is turned into an order of life for the dormitory Aborigines, and in a way they have no linguistic option before them because elimination of the native languages is also a kind of infliction of extreme silence. It is not just thrusting English on them but, inevitably, also moulding their English to Queen's English to avoid any possible Aboriginal features. Glenyse Ward's *Unna You Fullas* brilliantly reflects this by referring to her dormitory and school experiences and how Aboriginal children were strictly ordered not to use words like "nah," "unna," "fullas" etc. because, according to the teacher, they are all strange Aboriginal words, but not English. When one's language is eliminated or cannot be spoken, that itself is a great loss to a person and it is a kind of silencing. There is every chance of that person voluntarily taking up silence either because of grief over the loss of one's own language, or because of an inability to learn an alternative or simply because giving up one's language and taking up another is a compulsion. It affects all the more when one is forced to give up one's language and take up another and that too in the standard form. This contributes all the more to the silencing of the person. This is exactly what we come across in the situation presented by Aboriginal women writers, in particular, Glenyse Ward.

It is also interesting how Ward brings to our notice the attempts of German missionaries to speak English and how the Aboriginal children laughed at them, secretly of course, about the heavy German accent. It is interesting because a group that has lost its language, that has taken to another language and is being ordered to use it correctly, laughs at the attempts of another non-English speaking group and its attempts to get Anglicised in speech and action.

It is all the more intriguing when we look into the reasons for this silence employed by Aboriginal women writers. Rita Huggins, in *Auntie Rita*, says that it is difficult to voice those experiences because of a sense of shame and pain. Still, the reason behind this silence is always somewhat enigmatic, as it has to be, for it is this enigmatic quality that gives rise to multiple interpretations of the text. For instance, there are silences in Sally Morgan's *My Place* and Monica Clare's *Karobran*. At a given place it may be a partial silence like just referring to the issue but not giving much importance or not dwelling on it in long discussions. At another place it may be complete silence over a particular issue, which we know does exist. Both these kinds of cases speak eloquently about the silence employed by Aboriginal women writers, and above all they speak in multiple voices depending on the multiple interpretations of the readers. Aileen Moreton-Robinson rightly observes,

> It is no mere coincidence that Indigenous and white men are not mentioned or featured as main characters in the texts; it is Indigenous women's relations with other Indigenous women that are given significance. . . . However, it is more likely that sexuality is kept private or accorded little attention because this is where Indigenous women have drawn the boundary between themselves and their audience. A boundary that is related to the way in which cultural processes have shaped their subjectivity. (15-16)

Apart from finding it painful and shameful to narrate those experiences, Aboriginal women resent expressing their pain and feelings to the whites or non-Aboriginal readers. Glenyse Ward's *Unna You Fullas* brilliantly portrays repressive dormitories and rebellious Aboriginal girls. The runaway girls—Banner, Thelma, Zelda, Nickey and Bella—unfortunately fail to escape from the long arms of the Mission and are brought back to the Mission. Banner, who leads the group and who does not repent for her running away from the home, gets the worst beating by Fr. Albertus. The inmates of the home are shocked and some of them burst out but Banner bears it silently: "I didn't want to let them know I was in pain, I didn't want them to see me crying" (Ward 1991: 87). It is this self-esteem that takes the form of or finds expression in silence. But this silence is also the result of Banner's hatred for Fr. Albertus and when he meets with a fire accident while he is gardening, Banner is with him, still, and yet silent. She seems to be uninvolved in the whole episode, but her involvement cannot be denied. Thus the repressed feelings and reactions find their "expression," so to say, in the *noticeably* silent protest.

As against the background of such autobiographies and their strategy of responding to discrimination, Glenyse Ward's *Wandering Girl* comes to us in a different light. She does not overtly protest against racial discrimination but rather simply narrates her terrible experiences describing her painful predicament. Her "innocent" narration in itself is her strategy of protest and resistance. Her autobiography does not deconstruct any established image but tries to construct the life of a slave girl so as to speak for itself. This involves the reader, compelling him to draw the unstated conclusion. Her ignorance of the general predicament of the Aborigines and her innocence and implicit acceptance of racial inferiority powerfully construct the life and servile identity of an average Aborigine. Her being unaware of the Aboriginal movement itself turns out to be an asset to her implicit argument. Her autobiography does not consciously replace white history but it does reflect the fate of the whole enslaved community of Aborigines. What Sally Morgan states in *My Place*, the instances of Aboriginal children removed from their parents and culture, finds a link in other autobiographies and reaches the readers in its ultimate destiny in Ward's *Wandering Girl.*

Wandering Girl is one of the Aboriginal women's autobiographies that give a hint of class conflict to the whole issue of white versus native. She seems to concentrate on how an upper class family exploited her as a slave girl, though her being an Aborigine is one of the reasons for her life in the Board and her career as a slave. This is not completely ignored by the writer. Her autobiography concludes with the end of her career as a slave, except for a brief epilogue when she was free and happy as a wife and mother in her later life. This also allows the naïve narration to turn into a very strong attack against discrimination and injustice. Her selection of a particular period in her life as the theme of her autobiography vehemently highlights the very notion of discrimination, and it makes us feel, not merely understand, that enslaved Aborigines had no genuine existence or identity. Without spelling it out, she manages to fight against Aboriginal slavery in the very theme of her autobiography. She often refers to the oppressors as white bosses and implicitly suggests that their authority had to be accepted without questioning. But she subtly and covertly questions every aspect of white supremacy over blacks by delineating the pathetic plight of blacks:

> Soon as I opened the door all the chatter and laughter stopped. You could hear a pin drop as all eyes were on me. All of a sudden, some poshed-up voice, with a plum in her mouth, came out of the crowd, "Tracey dear, is this your little dark servant?"

> I just stood there smiling. I thought it was wonderful that at last people were taking notice of me. There were sniggers and jeers from everywhere. I turned to the lady who did all the talking, and said, "My name is Glenyse." She was quite startled; she said, "Oh dear, I didn't think you had a name." (Ward 1987: 24)

The unmistakable yet unvoiced protest in Ward's book makes it distinct from some of the overtly protesting autobiographies. Disobeying her mistress' orders that she should not appear before the guests, Glenyse Ward suddenly barges into the party and her very identity as a human being is simultaneously denied and questioned as well as forcefully asserted here. Glenyse Ward seems to admit this innocently but the narration is enough to infuriate the readers. One cannot but conclude that this is one of the most brilliant, even if unintentional, strategies of Glenyse Ward to protest against racist discrimination and to assert herself far more effectively than an outburst could.

It is noteworthy that Deborah Bird Rose calls this silence a meta-communication. Holding back of information, refusal to share information, which is also a form of silence but a constructive silence, silence used as a strategy, are the forms of silence that we find in Aboriginal women's writing. Jackie Huggins, in her *Sister Girl*, rightly points out:

> The constant demands placed on Aboriginal people to be the educators is tiring. Surely it is time for non-Aboriginal people to begin their journey of discovery by themselves. It is too much to expect Aboriginal people to be continually explaining their oppression—as if somehow it is their fault and they have to talk and write their way out of it. And do others really listen to their pleas? (1998 x)

Although these words provide a clue to the silence in Aboriginal women's writing, they also raise some questions. For instance, does it not contradict the argument that so far only whites have been writing about Aborigines? No doubt Huggins' words mirror the reality and more so the question that is posed at the end of the above statement. But, it is one of the major concerns of Aboriginal literature that, while so far only whites have written about indigenous people it is time for the indigenous people to speak about themselves and the oppression that they have been subjected to. Probably this is the dilemma that all marginalised literatures and silenced voices experience as there is an indignation about others writing about them and simultaneously about expectations of others for them to speak "for themselves." As an imposed silence conditions and kills individuality, a compelled eloquence also conditions and stifles expression.

The conditioning of the Aboriginal women to be silent thus works in two ways as it has been discussed earlier. There is a requirement ordered by the entire social institution of Australia to be silent and there is also a requirement from their Aboriginal identity and Aboriginal society that they should be silent about their pain and pleasure. Thus they are conditioned to be silent in two ways by two forces, but one destructive and the other constructive, or at least preservative. Jackie Huggins observes, "I came to understand that the resistance that Aboriginal people meet in white bureaucrats when attempting to see Aboriginal records is one of the most contemporary forms that silencing takes" (1998 132).

Silence that is used as a strategy of protest and which is a consequence of conditioning also puts forth some questions: is this protest naïve, is it conscious, and is this eloquence of silence intended or unintended? Who are these writers addressing themselves to, whites or their fellow indigenous people, or indigenous women in particular? For instance, Jackie Huggins says in *Auntie Rita* suggesting self-consciousness:

> One of the most important things Aboriginal people can do for their children is to instil a dignified purpose and strong identity of being Aboriginal. This is the foundation for their future and costs nothing. It is a duty we all have to ourselves and our next generations. To be proud to say who we are and what we are without any feeling of inferiority is one of the greatest gifts of life we can give to our children. A secure identity base is the basic ingredient for the hazardous road ahead. (Huggins and Huggins 101)

If the writer is addressing herself to indigenous people, as it is quite evident in these two cases at least, how does her silence about certain issues help her and her readers? For it deprives her of the opportunity of sharing her experiences. Does it help since problems and suffering are understood by others because they too go through similar predicaments? If she is addressing the whites, how does such information and tone reach them and how does she intend them to react? How can she be sure they will notice the content or the tone? As Jackie Huggins observes,

> Until there is a real understanding of racism in this country and genuine moves made towards racial equality, many Aboriginal women will not be prepared to talk publicly, to audiences of "others," about the oppression they suffer through sexism. White feminists' interference in this issue is unwelcome, as to date it has only reinforced racist stereotypes of Aboriginal women, men and culture. (1998: 35)

There is silence between the characters and besides that is the silence between the writer and the readers. Silence between the Aboriginal and white characters may be of a kind that was inflicted. But the silence that exists between the writer and the readers is the one that was, at least in some cases, intended. For Aboriginal women writers make brilliant use of the right to give or withhold information that the writers feel entitled to. Monica Clare's complete silence about her first marriage and her child through this marriage is one of the best examples of this. We see Isabelle as a girl first, and then suddenly she comes to us as a woman. What happened in between we do not know unless we read the Introduction.

This silence may also be related to the interference of a few members of the dominant community in the name of editing and publishing. Having a coloniser as editor or publisher for writing about the coloniser's exploitative behaviour and legacy may be expected to have its own corrupting or softening or adverse impact on the narrative. Consider a situation in which an Aboriginal is verbally narrating and expects to be represented in writing by an editor; or a situation in which an Aboriginal's writing is considered in need of 'improvement' by himself or by an editor, or by both. In this kind of situation, statements may end up being distorted, and even silences on the part of the narrator/writer may end up being distorted or losing their point or force. First, the editor or the publisher may want the writer to be selective about memory or oblivion even when the writer does not. Secondly, the writer herself may hold back information. There may be, in this phenomenon, other factors also such as sense of shame and pain, hesitation, fear of betrayal, doubt about reaction to revelations. There may also be an order of priorities for the writer which may urge her to be silent or eloquent on particular issues and situations. Indeed, silences may point to, eloquently, what caused them. Thus, the intermediary whom the writer intends to assign the task of reaching out may end up corrupting or weakening the silence, or the eloquence, or the eloquent silence in the text. Aileen Moreton-Robinson converts for us this possibility of corrupting significant silence, into an argument about texts and subtexts:

> Literary relations such as these are representative of power relations between coloniser and colonised. Indigenous women's knowledge in itself cannot be accommodated, but must be redefined to conform to the requirements of white literary practice. However, although white editing or scribing may influence the writing of the text, it does not erase the subtext, which is informed by the knowledge and experience of Indigenous women. (2)

Moreton-Robinson raises, in fact, a fundamental matter here. No doubt, writing is basically an act of communication. Yet, no communication can be complete and perfect, either. Indeed, there are bound to be missing links in any writing, depending on the writer's purpose and familiarity of the readers with the writer's world. But, there are occasions when such a missing link becomes prominent, thrusts its absence upon the reader. For instance, there are obvious silences caused by age-old oppression and colonisation in writings on the subject. Personal and sexual oppression to which Australian Aboriginal people have been subjected for centuries will automatically raise expectations among readers that representation of these or such topics will occur in them. However, as we have seen earlier in the chapter, these issues either become focal points in Aboriginal women's autobiographies or are significantly absent. As we saw earlier in the case of Monica Clare and Sally Morgan, for instance, there are certain gaps that one cannot but notice in their narratives.

These absences are a major factor in the field of writing by oppressed people in particular. Like the black cloth on a cage that covers a pet parrot, such absence raises readers' curiosity about the missing links. It is like putting up a signboard announcing a town farther along but without a road laid to reach it. Ironically, therefore, you can neither miss it nor find it! This is where absence becomes presence and silence speaks loudly.

Such missing yet "announced" subject matter becomes especially intriguing and powerful in situations that generally prevent or discourage expression. This is the case of Australian Aboriginal literature in general and it is unmistakably the case of women's writing. Now, what happens to a reader when he encounters such "speaking" missing links? He must wonder what the writer might have communicated. When the reader belongs to the 'oppressing' community, he may also feel a sense of guilt. Here our aim is to establish this provocative situation in our chosen field of study.

In this context, Stepehen Muecke's "Repressive Hypothesis" is a good example of how, not frequently, the principal text remained with Aboriginal people whereas only a sub-text was available to readers. Further, Aboriginal writers have the choice to decide which subtext may be offered to readers. For instance, withholding information and experience was the strategy that many Aboriginal women writers adopted to protect the text that they might have wished to convey only to Aboriginal readers. Thus, one way or another it may not have been the same text that reached the non-indigenous and the indigenous readership. As Jackie Huggins points out in *Sister Girl*, from which we also quoted in the Introduction while discussing Aboriginal theatre, that no Aboriginal text should be completely accessible to non-indigenous readers; such is the view of at least many an Aboriginal writer. Similarly, while discussing the white intrusion and demand to speak, Stephen Muecke points out:

> But in the face of this powerful demand, could it be the case that Aboriginal people have learnt to retain a judicious silence, only giving out a certain amount of carefully constructed discourse, making sure we are aware that in their economy of discourses the

> first separation is between the "public" and the "secret" and that a great wealth of culture lies below the surface? (411)

However, this judicious silence may not be a result of a choice of the writer/composer in cases where texts are translated or transcribed by non-indigenous persons; for in such cases considerable interference may be perceived, and this may lead to distortion and curtailment of intended expression. Transcription of oral literature provides the best example for this. On the other hand, the text may not be available either to non-indigenous or to indigenous readers because it is intended to be hidden from the non-indigenous mediator. Yet even in this case, what is not said can at times convey the intended message to the Aboriginal people who have similar experiences to those regarding which silence is maintained. Here, silence is no longer mute but becomes a message and turns out to be significant discourse.

Consider a specific example of such selective silence from a different context, for instance, Native Canadian literature: Florence Edenshaw's autobiography as told to Margaret Blackman, *During My Time: Florence Edenshaw Davidson—A Haida Woman* (1982), presents a good case of coexistence of overt text and subtext perhaps unavailable to Anglophone or Francophone readers, but not necessarily to indigenous readers. Blackman in her preface to the Revised Edition (1992) herself says that Florence's account was subject to a number of cultural constraints. Issues of cultural representation and representation of self are crucial in Northwest Coast Canadian societies. Blackman says, "Florence's own editorial hand in her life history was apparent from the very beginning. 'I don't tell everything—what's no good' she cautioned. . . . On more than one occasion, she would instruct me to 'shut that things off' [sic] while she related something important that was not to be included in the book" (xiii). This gives an impression that the published work is solely the writer's (narrator's) text. But, after a few pages, in the chapter titled "The Life History Project," Blackman confesses that to a large extent her own interest biased the life-history data she obtained. This completely dismantles the concept of the narrator's text that she had earlier constructed. Anyway, the narrator has adopted her own ways of silence and eloquence as the mediator has her own. That way, the text that the narrator wanted to convey was partly "selected" by the mediator even though the narrator had a say in selecting parts of the narrative.

Such eloquent silences also raise questions about the very form of autobiography. If the writer's intention is to write an autobiography as a community experience, how does this silence help? How to relate the silence of the writer as an individual to the writer as a writer or as an individual who comes forward to talk to the readers about her life? If the Aboriginal writer is talking to her own people, is the detailed discussion of customs, traditions and lifestyle only a sharing or is it also a mode of informing? When the same details are also available to the whites, how is this purpose of sharing fulfilled? Does one narrative have two or even more functions and two achievements at two levels, of sharing with indigenous people and of informing non-indigenous people? How does the same narrative become silent at one place, that is, to some readers, and eloquent at some other places to others? Some of these questions have already been addressed in the Introduction while discussing the use of Aboriginal English in Aboriginal theatre. This discussion focused on the strategy of use of English so as to remain partly incomprehensible to non-indigenous people. The section on silence in Aboriginal women's autobiographies earlier in the present chapter has also discussed some of these issues at length. However, there are larger or specific questions that need to be addressed keeping in mind not only the genre, but also the particular social, political and cultural context of the texts. An attempt is made to address some of these questions in discussing of individual works in the later chapters.

If absolute silence about some aspects of life is a prominent feature of these autobiographies, a strong urge to reveal and share, a typical feature of story telling, can also be perceived in Aboriginal women's autobiographies. Be it a description of cooking, beliefs, customs, routine—whatever may be the topic, we feel that the writers are educating the readers or sharing with them, taking them into confidence. The frequent use of "we" instead of "I" and the very personal note of addressing the reader, create a collective experience since the writer gives an impression of directly addressing the reader.

Literature is used here as a force by Aboriginal women writers to narrate the facts and express their anger and protest. It is quite clear that their battle is against racial discrimination. Loss and awareness of the loss are other important themes in their attack on racial discrimination. Their loss started with the loss of land, extended gradually via loss of livelihood, culture, motherhood, justice and reached the point of loss of identity. Ngûgî wa Thiong'o's words about "mental control" can be extrapolated and used in this context:

> For colonialism this involved two aspects of the same process: the destruction or the deliberate undervaluing of a people's culture, their art, dances, religions, history, geography, education, orature and literature, and the conscious elevation of the language of the coloniser. The domination of a people's language by the languages of the colonising nations was crucial to the domination of the mental universe of the colonised. (16)

It is the complete loss that the Africans have suffered that is voiced by Ngûgî. A similar kind of loss the Aborigines have suffered in Australia and are trying to protest against it. They may not be able to bring back the glorious past in spite of any number or kinds of attempts but they will definitely be able to assert that the colonised past was atrocious. They will be able to change the course of the future at least.

Let us look at the concept of loss from the perspective of Aborigines. They have, according to their literature, never believed in the ownership of land. For them, it was the land that owned them. Probably that is one of the reasons for their not demanding that the whites leave their country. They have always believed that they are only the custodians of the land. Before they could understand the nuances of the white man's concept of land ownership, they had lost their sacred earth. Thus nostalgia for the loss of land is one of the themes of Aboriginal literature in general and women's autobiographies in particular.

They have lost their culture along with the land. Roberta Sykes says that the white man entered with the Bible in one hand and a sword in another. He gave the Bible to the Aborigines and used the sword against them. With the loss of their identity as free human beings, the colonisation was complete. They remained slaves in every sense of the term and nothing was left which they could call their own. That they had no citizenship rights in Australia till 1967 is the best example for their enslavement. Loss of motherhood, as it was discussed earlier, had a multi-dimensional effect on the Aborigines. First, mothers were bewildered as their children were separated from them, a practice which was unknown to them earlier. Children became dispossessed orphans as they had no parents, no language, no religion, and no tribe of their own. Thus it caused harassment of women, alienation of children and elimination of Aboriginal culture, language, religion and Aboriginal consciousness. This is firmly resisted by these women writers. Some of them produce witnesses to such ghastly experiences. For instance, Sally Morgan finds out that her grandmother has another daughter apart from her mother and that the grandmother does not know the whereabouts of her daughter and vice versa. She also comes to know the horrendous fact about the incest, that Sally Morgan's grandmother and her mother were fathered by the same white man.

Behind all these issues such as loss, discrimination and exploitation lies one principle, that is, injustice. Their protest is against the injustice inflicted upon them and they do not express any contempt for the whites as a race but only look forward to reconciliation on the basis of equality. It is not only the liberation of the self but an effort towards the liberation of the race. Aborigines, as a race, are imprisoned and it is not only the oppressive past that haunts them; the suppressing present and the threatening future also bewilder them. Autobiography becomes a vehicle to express a longing of the race as well as a longing of the self for freedom.

Multiple Voices of the Writer

Since autobiography is a biography of the self, the very first question that emerges while reading or analysing an autobiography concerns the way the writer perceives herself in her autobiography. When it comes to the question of autobiographies of Australian Aboriginal women, the above question becomes more prominent and crucial, because their autobiographies revolve around the issue of identity and raise questions and controversies about it. This chapter will discuss how this self is contemplated and expressed and analyse the factors that condition the thought and expression in Aboriginal women's autobiographies.

From this crucial predicament and issue of identity emanate the multiple voices of the Aboriginal woman writer. These voices represent the dominating consciousness of the writer as it is expressed in her autobiography and also the identity of the writer according to herself. As the discourse of identity gets emphasised in these autobiographies, the question of the writer's identity or the concept of her consciousness also becomes complex. In some of Australian Aboriginal women's autobiographies, the consciousness of gender dominates, whereas in some others the consciousness of race. Apart from this, we also come across the consciousness of the Aboriginal woman, which is quite authentic and operative in deciding the identity of the writer's predicament as a colonised. Both the terms in the phrase "Aboriginal woman" are very significant, individually and together and this Aboriginal woman's consciousness is the most crucial feature of these autobiographies. This chapter will discuss how the multiple voices of the Aboriginal women's autobiographies represent the writers' concerns and purposes, simultaneously or distinctly.

Although this chapter uses consciousness and voice as synonymous terms at places, that is not an attempt to say that both are one and the same. But the voices of Aboriginal women reflect the consciousness that they have or the consciousness or identity that dominates their being. In other words, the voices of the writers vary on the basis of their identity according to themselves and according to the society in which they exist. But this consciousness may not always find a voice or may get transformed into the consciousness of one of the multiple identities that are independent and interconnected. Their writings need to be approached by readers and critics with varying expectations, depending on the identity of the writers and the purpose of their writing.

It is not always easy to determine whether a particular voice represents gender consciousness or racial consciousness. A thorough understanding of these autobiographies and the socio-cultural and historical milieu is required in order to hear the multiple voices of the writers. This knowledge will certainly introduce the background to the Aboriginal predicament though it may not give a definite picture. Although these autobiographies give the readers an impression of being "autoethnographies," these writers do present individual cases as well, since they come from different individual backgrounds and situations. It also becomes difficult to decide on these writers' voices and consciousness since they are interconnected very closely. Sometimes a writer reveals that it is her Aboriginal consciousness that is predominant in her autobiography but the text unveils something else, or the writer wishes to say something else, but her writing discloses her Aboriginal consciousness.

Let us consider, for instance, the case of Roberta Sykes. Concerning her, as also several other writers, there appears to be some uncertainty regarding whether she is genuinely black. But, as the case with Mudrooroo Narogin, her ideas and theirs may still help us in the context. (See the following chapter for a brief discussion of this controversy.) For example, she declares that she looks at herself as a black woman (Personal Interview 9 January 1998). The title of her autobiography, *Snake Dreaming: Autobiography of a Black Woman*, also makes this clear. Although she puts it very clearly that she looks at herself as a black woman, several questions arise in this context: What is her social, economic, intellectual, political, psychological and historical status as a black woman? Is she a rural/tribal or an urban/ urbanised black woman? Do such factors independently or collectively play a crucial role in moulding her voice? Can a black woman be as simple a term as it sounds and a definition of Aboriginal woman? If that is her identity according to herself, what is her identity in the eyes of "her" society and according to white society? (Indeed, whether or not a person belongs to a certain race may be a tricky issue to resolve. Meanwhile, if that person feels her racial identity and has been treated by others on the basis of that identity, for our purposes her views may be treated as authentic within reason. For more on this subject of identity, look at the following chapter.) What is the consciousness/ voice that is heard in her writings, not only according to her but also according to her readers and critics?

Several such fundamental questions and different arguments of the various Aboriginal writers raise many other questions which may also be problematic in the context of racial authenticity or authenticity of representation. For instance, Sally Morgan has been questioned regarding her representation of Aboriginality. And she does speak in different voices in different contexts. Her autobiography *My Place* was a tremendous success, became a trendsetter and was followed by many Aboriginal women's autobiographies. In *My Place*, Aboriginal consciousness and the issue of Aboriginal identity find prominent place. It is a direct and overt representation of Aboriginal predicament, history, culture, dilemma, identity, consciousness and her search for roots. In fact, the whole autobiography revolves around the issues of going back to the roots, digging up "history" and reconstructing the history of Aboriginal people. That she includes the stories of her mother, grandmother and grandmother's brother in her autobiography provides evidence to Sally Morgan's anxiety to make as many Aboriginal voices audible as possible to readers and to represent Aboriginal life as intimately as possible. In fact, she herself admits: "What had begun as a tentative search for knowledge had grown into a spiritual and emotional pilgrimage. We had an Aboriginal consciousness now, and were proud of it" (Morgan 233). The knowledge she refers to is knowledge about her Aboriginal roots and the place of her belonging. She describes this search as a spiritual and emotional pilgrimage, implying her immense respect for Aboriginal culture.

The interrogating autobiography of Sally Morgan raises several issues starting from the writer's identity, her roots and her identity dilemmas, all of which seem to have cropped up in her own writing or in interviews; especially, when questioned, blurred, or denied certain aspects of identity, one is forced to speak of or write about. It is not unlikely, in fact, that a writer who takes on such a subject may end up with some queries or unanswered objections regarding either a given aspect of her identity or the co-existence of several aspects. While we must be critical in evaluating such problems of clash or confusion among different identities, we can hardly deny that the situation itself is more complex than for someone well-settled in their community and whose community is not beleaguered by questions of identity. One cannot, therefore, expect an Aboriginal writer's work to be altogether free from such confusion or even conflict in a postcolonially heightened state of self-consciousness. Morgan's work presents us with a very good example of this far-from-clear predicament of someone attempting to re-locate themselves.

As we shall also see later in our discussion on multiple identities, *My Place* brings up very personal questions about the writer, in the process exploring and exposing larger issues like racial discrimination, physical torment, mental trauma, gender bias and politics in the name of welfare. Her dilemma over her receiving the Aboriginal fellowship regarding how Aboriginal she is does not remain a mere personal question but extends to the whole Aboriginal situation, evokes debates about the definition of "Aboriginality." It also asserts her Aboriginal lineage. Her going back to her Aboriginal roots also holds a mirror up to the situation, where Aboriginal people are opening up, crossing the threshold of their sense of shame and pain and desperately going in search of their Aboriginal roots, and are, thus, also digging up the hidden histories of ghastly atrocities against their people and their ancestors.

Whether she is presenting her individual situation or commenting and contemplating on the general Aboriginal situation, it is the Aboriginal consciousness in Sally Morgan that speaks and not a general Australian consciousness. Like other marginalised writers, she acts as a representative of her race, not only of herself, whether it is in deconstructing the colonial history and reconstructing the alternative history or in expressing her righteous indignation at the absence of Aboriginal voices in Australian history and at the denial of access to Aboriginal people, to their own and their ancestors' records. Although different, both reinforce the need for Aboriginal people to know their history and to create their own. These aspects of *My Place* strongly express the Aboriginal argument to readers and the writer's Aboriginal consciousness and commitment towards Aboriginal issues make the text an out and out Aboriginal text.

Even as her autobiography published in 1987 comes to us as an Aboriginal text with an overtly Aboriginal consciousness and voice, Sally Morgan's interview with Delys Bird and Dennis Haskell in 1991 tries to present a different Sally Morgan with a completely contrasting voice. She presents a new reading of her text and herself as a writer by saying that she is one of those people who want to forget about what they, as Aboriginal people, had once experienced. If she wanted to forget or wants to forget what the Aboriginal people have gone through once, or are going through now, the text and the writer contradict each other. If oblivion, she thinks, is her stand, her excavation and reconstruction of history, her representation of Aboriginal voices and her concern for the past, present and future of Aboriginal history and culture set up a counterpoint to it.

My Place does not echo the sympathy of a mere outsider or a detached and distanced observer, but an identification with the community of suffering Aborigines. Her definition of the self may have changed by the time she gave her interview as an established writer, but her shift in her political stand is what poses the problem to the question of individual identity versus Aboriginal identity. This evokes the kind of questions that Roberta Sykes' statement about her identity raises. This also raises the question of different versions and interpretations that the writer and the text present and how the writer may distance the text from herself and herself from the text, even in an autobiography. Community consciousness and identity dominate over the personal or the individual identity and consciousness in many Aboriginal women's autobiographies. Under these circumstances, we may wonder which self the writer is distancing from the text and which text from the self. This will in a way determine the audible voice in a text like *My Place* and also in other Aboriginal women's autobiographies.

My Place brilliantly depicts, literally and metaphorically, the independent but interconnected journeys of three women. For Sally Morgan's grandmother, Daisy Corunna, it is a journey towards shedding her Aboriginal identity, because of which she is scared of white brutalities and separation from her family. For Sally's mother, Gladys Corunna, it is a lonely journey in life carrying the yoke of family responsibilities. For Sally, her journey of search for her identity gives both her and us an insight into the temporarily forgotten or longed to be forgotten identity. Thus, three voices representing three generations and three attitudes towards life speak to the reader in *My Place*. One voice, that of Daisy Corunna, represents the fear of the Aboriginal people of humiliation and ill-treatment from white society and government and their effort to hide their Aboriginal identity in order to lead their life in a "safe," "secure" and "respectable" manner. It is the voice of an Aboriginal woman who has been exploited, played with and who has been deprived of freedom, protection, community life and motherhood and who is being haunted by the threat of her Aboriginal identity being detected. Hence, her Aboriginal woman's voice becomes discreet but her Aboriginal consciousness and her Aboriginal response mark her character as an Aboriginal woman.

Her daughter Gladys Corunna represents the next generation—urbanised, self-reliant, even married to a white man; she has a family of her own, and she is institutionalised like all colonised people are, but not to the same extent as her mother is. Whether she is tormented by the threat of her Aboriginal identity being detected or not, her womanhood, to be specific, her wifehood, becomes a source of suffering for her. Her white husband returns from the battlefield and converts their house and life into a battlefield with his post-war trauma. Her husband's death releases her from that battlefield and she takes on the role of a young widow with the whole family relying on her. Whether she has any opportunity to feel nostalgic about her Aboriginal heritage and brood over its loss or not, her consciousness as a woman with responsibilities and duties does not allow her to think about or express it. It is predominantly a woman's voice that reaches the readers in Sally Morgan's mother.

Although these three women come from the same family, they hail from and are rooted in different locations and these determine their voices. They live with the identity of Indians—Sally's grandmother construes it; Sally's mother remains a spectator in that identity crisis; while Sally herself acquires or rather is given this identity. All these women enter into a discourse with the readers in different voices—of the Aboriginal, the woman and the Aboriginal woman. As we have seen in the case of Roberta Sykes also, even these three identities are associated with the writer's social, economic, political, intellectual, historical and cultural locations and contexts.

In general, all these three voices speak in this autobiography with sensitivity to the gender issue. They realise or are conscious that their identity as women adds to the difficulties that they face, that they are doubly exploited as Aborigines and women and of course as Aboriginal women too. This gender discrimination is not confined to white society but extends to the urban Aboriginal families as well. Sally Morgan does not ignore this aspect of Aboriginal life. She looks at the tough situation from a multidimensional perspective. Her paternal grandparents and her father, who are white, and her maternal grandmother and mother, who face life with the untiring spirit of soldiers—everyone wants a male heir. Sally Morgan recollects: "Nan had always favoured the boys in our family, and now Dad was doing the same" (48). Even Sally Morgan's mother, who was never happy and secure in the company of her white husband, looks forward to a man being the head of the family: "A couple of weeks after Dad had died, Mum informed us all that Billy was now the man of the house. This came as a great surprise to me, because Billy was only six years old" (50). In her paternal grandparents' attitude, Sally Morgan perceives discrimination not only of race but also of gender: "The only one of us they were really keen on was Billy, and that was only because he was the image of Dad. Grandpa always liked to have Billy close to him, but the rest of us were relegated to the backyard. Our cousins were allowed inside, but we had to stay outside" (52). Thus Sally Morgan and her sister, being women of Aboriginal descent, suffer discrimination within as well as outside the family. That a male heir is preferred both by her mother and grandmother and her white grandparents raises questions about her female identity and discrimination against women. Although she does not feel frustrated or depressed about it, she becomes conscious of the gender inequalities and that paves the road for her self-representation as a woman.

Speaking to the readers in these three interconnected and indistinguishable voices of woman, Aborigine, and Aboriginal woman in her autobiography, Sally Morgan reveals in her interview that the consciousness from which her autobiography emerges is "very much working class, you wouldn't have called us anything else; 'poor working class' would probably be more appropriate" (Bird and Haskell 7). This adds one more strand to Sally Morgan's identity and one more consciousness to her autobiography. Whether Sally Morgan's autobiography has working class consciousness and the readers understand her as a representative of the "poor working class" in her autobiography or not, some of the other Aboriginal women's autobiographies do not miss this aspect of Aboriginal life in a colonial situation.

Glenyse Ward's *Wandering Girl* is one of the autobiographies in which the working class consciousness dominates the consciousness of race and gender. Straight from Saint Joseph's orphanage at Rivervale, Glenyse reaches Bigelow's house as a domestic. Brought up in a strict environment where she was taught never to speak out to people unless she was spoken to first, no matter what the circumstances were, she quietly receives the old tin mug that she has to use for drinking tea. As a dark servant of a rich household she is overburdened with a long list of chores. It is not that she completely lacks awareness of her plight. She knows that race and class are responsible for her predicament. She recollects: "I couldn't get wild, because they were white people and our bosses. What could we do? Nothing!" (Ward 1987: 115). And, "In those days, not so long either, we were not allowed to say anything against our white bosses" (*ibid.* 126).

Although she refers to "white bosses," the readers get the impression that it is not only a question of racial difference but also the class difference that determines their predicament. There is an acceptance on her part of her predicament and an effort to convince herself that she must accept her plight as a black domestic. There is, apparently, not even a streak of covert protest in her behaviour or demeanour. It is not that she does not get angry or feel like bursting out against her boss, but she is not allowed to do that. Her statements quoted above not only reveal her understanding and acceptance of the situation but also accommodate several unarticulated and unanswered questions about power relations in a colonised society.

Although she expresses her fear as bottled up by her helplessness, she does not remain completely passive and subservient, but protests in her own way. Although told not to appear before the guests, she walks straight into the party surprising the guests and infuriating her mistress. In another instance, scared of going into the orchard, Glenyse Ward squeezes the stored fruits, violating the order of her mistress to be served fresh fruit juice. Tea in the old tin mug and some oats are all that is allotted to her whereas in her mistress's absence Glenyse Ward eats the food "meant for the whites" in their party ware. She enjoys the luxuries of her mistress's bedroom. Above all, Glenyse Ward takes an unexpected route on her way to the mission for a holiday. This bold step transforms her life from that of slavery to liberty.

Her protest does not find verbal expression but manifests itself in action. Although silent and covert, her protest underlines her comments about differences and discrimination. Whether her Aboriginal consciousness comes out in her protest or not, her working class-consciousness does spring up in her silent yet powerful protest against economically, socially, politically and culturally "superior" people.

In *Unna You Fullas,* Glenyse Ward once again comes to the readers as a dormitory girl. A similar acceptance of the predicament and silent protest characterise this consciousness of a dormitory girl. Here, it seems to be her identity as a dormitory girl, not even her identity as a stolen child, which comes forth. Although questions of stolen generation and dormitory life are not completely distinct and unconnected with each other, Glenyse Ward does not discuss the issue of the stolen generation much, and she does not identify herself either as a stolen child or with the fellow dormitory girls who try to escape from the travails of dormitory life. Unlike other Aboriginal women writers and other dormitory girls, she "owns" the dormitory and thinks that the dormitory "owns" her like a home. However, it is true in a way that she is owned by the institution through its power and discrimination, but not through its love and care as she assumes. She thinks that the dormitory is her home and the Sisters and the Brothers of the German Mission are her parents. Since she was removed from her parents when she was very young, as she herself reveals, she is unable to view herself as a dispossessed, dislocated and displaced stolen child. She cannot visualise her lost home, parents, society and culture. Although she believes and tries hard to convince herself that the Mission is her home and she belongs there, every now and then the protests and revolts by the fellow inmates create storms in her mind. Their tears over her innocence and her predicament as a stolen child faintly shake the foundation of her belief and this reverberates through her writing to her readers.

Glenyse Ward is thus torn between her conditioning and her growing up mind. Her complexion, features, Aboriginal English, common dress, dormitory life and the treatment meted out to her reiterate her Aboriginal identity. But her attachment to the Mission drags her to the other side. Thus the voice that emanates from the dilemma of Aboriginal stolen children turns into a voice that speaks with uncertainties and vacillation about her identity. It is the sense of belonging, which is a crucial and decisive issue in Aboriginal culture that decides the identity of Glenyse Ward here. In *Unna You Fullas*, Glenyse Ward remains a faithful and accommodative dormitory girl with occasional streaks of protest. But, in *Wandering Girl*, as the title itself speaks about her concept of her identity, directly or ironically, she turns into a black domestic with strong roots in her dormitory life, which demanded absolute silence and passivity.

As Jackie Huggins rightly observes, "In the colonial context, the Black man had virtually lost his bargaining powers and the coloniser assumed almost total control; hence, the interaction between white man and Black woman was one marked by compulsion" (1998: 14). Thus Aboriginal life was completely ruled by whites, giving rise to the awful phenomenon of the stolen generation. Aboriginal helplessness and absence of rights over their own life and their future were facts of the times. Ruth Hegarty says that this book would tell us about the hurt and pain that the girls suffered being separated from mothers and families. It has to be remembered that most girls in the dormitory already had only single parents. This again is the consequence of colonisation, which resulted in divisions such as "half-caste," "quarter-caste" and "part-Aboriginal." Because of the presence of white blood in them, according to the whites, they were more educable and hence were able to rapidly assimilate into white society. Whether assimilation into white society occurred or not, they were certainly alienated from their own culture and people. They were deprived of community life, love and warmth of parents, care and protection of their people and were trained to become no more than good domestics.

Ruth Hegarty's mother's life gets repeated in Ruth Hegarty's life. Her mother is deprived of motherhood and Ruth Hegarty also goes through a similar predicament. The re-enacted past unites these two women not only as mother and daughter but also as two Aboriginal women who went through similar exploitation at the hands of a discriminating society and government. Two mature women recollect, relive and reconstruct their past: "We are now two mature women, both mothers, reliving our past, and talking about painful times we had not really discussed before" (Hegarty 28). Both are deprived mothers. Both had been single parents. Both were silenced at a crucial period of their lives. Is this book not an outlet for their suppressed and silenced feelings and experiences? If so, what gives them the courage to open up their changed roles—maturity, freedom from dormitory or freedom from sense of shame and pain? And, what silenced them in the past—the government policies, dormitory life, fear, or self-esteem?

As Ruth Hegarty rightly puts it, it is opening up a closed chapter. But the question about this closed chapter is, was it ever really closed or is it being expanded into the present? If it is a community experience, is it really a closed chapter for every member? Who or what closed it—time, individuals or change in the discriminatory policies? The whole book seems to be a juxtaposition of then and now, past and present, childhood and adulthood, dormitory life and free life. The major difference between then and now is that the mother and daughter are together and they are able to open up to each other, which they had never done before: "We never talked about it among ourselves at that time. But now we are adults, without a threat of punishment or a sense of shame hanging over our heads, we are able to discuss these events quite openly" (Hegarty 77).

Ruth Hegarty's statements reveal the historicity of personality, experience and review. For instance, that she is a different person now or that at least she is attempting to prove that she is a different person. A whole set of such topics presents itself to our view once we recognise and acknowledge that an individual also is subject to historicity. Take the fact that this autobiography takes the form of an adult's point of view of her childhood. What food for thought such a retrospective form would provide? For example, even though the writer says that there is a change in her personality, surroundings and situation, still some questions may remain for the reader, such as whether the autobiography is a faithful reconstruction or reliving or fictionalisation. Questions about the functions that such narrative techniques perform in the book; whether the writers' recollection is from the point of view of an adult or recollecting and reconstructing as a free adult; what may be the purpose of such reconstruction, expression of nostalgia, fear and hatred that filled her childhood or adult effort at "understanding" etc.

Although Ruth Hegarty attempts to emphasise that she is a different person now, that does not seem to be completely true. For, clearly, she is what her past has made her. Neither can she delete the past from her life nor can she escape from the impact of that haunting past. For instance, she relates her present obsession with food to her starvation in the past, and says that her conditioned childhood results in disciplining her children or being conscious about her conditioning her children. Even the endearing call, "Is that you Ruthie?" reminds her of a call for punishment or a threat. As an adult she watches the children's film "The Wizard of Oz" on TV thirty years after she was denied a chance to watch the movie as a dormitory girl. Her autobiography is a recollection of childhood by an adult whose adulthood as well as its construction in the book are definitely moulded or influenced by her childhood. It is also an attempt to resist some of her childhood experiences. The haunting and conditioning memories remain a crucial part of her life and her childhood conditioning extends into adulthood and the sense of insecurity has its own role to play in it.

This story of conditioning and insecurity is also a story of deprivation. Ruth Hegarty's mother is deprived of education because her Aboriginal identity brings her humiliation from white children in school. Ruth Hegarty is deprived of her mother in the name of education. Both Ruth Hegarty and her mother are deprived of their children. Both Ruth Hegarty and her daughter, in turn, are deprived of their mothers. All the three are, like any other Aboriginal children, deprived of parental love, care, individuality, home and freedom in their institutionalised existence.

Even as Ruth Hegarty narrates the life of her mother, her mother narrates the most important episodes in her life; it is her mother who recollects why Ruth Hegarty started schooling at four and a half when other children started at five. She cries for other children and goes down to school to wait for them:

> I had no idea that this day was going to be the beginning of a long and sad separation. This day was to rob me of the natural bonding that existed between my mum and me, and would place me under the "care and protection" of the Queensland government, which now classified me as a neglected child. (Hegarty 26)

Thus her education deprives her of her mother. While her Aboriginal identity deprived Ruth Hegarty's mother of education, Ruth Hegarty is deprived of parental care in the name of education. In both the places, Aboriginal identity is what causes this deprivation, but for different reasons.

Ruth Hegarty's childhood is thus recollected and recreated by Ruth Hegarty's mother. Thus it is her mother's perspective, not hers that we perceive here. And we also perceive that Ruth Hegarty as an adult is herself listening to the narration of her childhood. She remains detached and an outsider as far as the episode of her going to school is concerned. But, surprisingly, she remembers every other incident that preceded or followed her school admission. Is it selective memory or does she want to listen to her mother's version and her agony of separation from her child?

This is evidence also of the vicious circle that led to the sexual exploitation of Aboriginal women by white men. Whether dormitory life resulted in single parentage or single parentage led to dormitory life is not debatable since clearly they were interrelated. Mother's day celebrations in the dormitory bring no joy to Aboriginal girls but only memories of their mothers and tears in their memory. The long-silenced agony has an outlet only in tears on Mother's day. Is this a celebration at all, is it an outlet or is the outlet an occasion for celebration?

A sense of loss and nostalgia permeate the lives of the dormitory girls and Ruth Hegarty becomes the spokesperson to convey them as her autobiography becomes her vehicle. The sense of loss gradually transforms itself into a sense of attachment to the dormitory. Ruth Hegarty says, "Even after the mistakes we were glad to go back to the dormitory, it became a haven of protection for us. It was hard to break away from a place that kept us dependent on it, and virtual prisoners" (93). This admission presents a paradoxical situation where the dormitory is both a haven and a jail for the Aboriginal girls. Paradoxical or not, the situation that she presents is pathetic and thought-provoking. The so-called mistakes that Ruth Hegarty refers to are the results of the Aboriginal identity of the dormitory girls. Many a time even if it was not the mistake of the girl at all, a punishment was imposed on her. Thus the guilty dormitory itself provides shelter for the girls who have been subjected to a heart-rending predicament in it because of their Aboriginal girl identity. It not only keeps them imprisoned as virtual prisoners, but it also compels the girls to depend on it once again and come back with shame and disgrace as single mothers. The tone of the book at this point sounds sarcastic at times as it refers to the dormitory as a haven of protection and also as a virtual jail. The use of the very word protection is ironic here for it is the last thing that was available to Aborigines colonised by whites. Indeed, it was in the name of protection that whites ruined the indigenous people and indigenous culture.

When Ruth Hegarty goes to a white household as a domestic, she does not forget the precautions she has to take as a grown up Aboriginal girl. She has her own room, her own toiletries and her own toilet, for which she had longed as a dormitory girl. But she still feels miserable as a domestic not only because she is treated even more badly by the white master and mistress, but also because she experiences terrible loneliness. She misses the voices of the children who formed one big family and the warmth of the dormitory and finds an emptiness, a deadness in her domestic situation. Definitely this is not a longing for the constrained dormitory life but a longing for the company of her fellow girls. She misses the community life that she had experienced as a child, the remnants of which she had experienced in the company of many other stolen children like her in the dormitory. She finds company in which she cannot share her happiness because she has no happiness. She finds company to share her woes silently and generate happiness from that deprivation and humiliation. She does not miss the menial jobs that she had to do in the dormitory like emptying the pots every morning, but she does miss her friends who accompany her to the toilet at night, braving the presumed existence of spirits. She does not miss the nightmare of going out alone at night but misses the peers who also suffer from the same nightmare which became worse for them in the absence of their people and parents.

If Glenyse Ward finds herself sandwiched or chooses to be sandwiched between her Aboriginal identity and dormitory girl identity, Ruth Hegarty puts forth a voice which is overt, direct, assertive and firm about her Aboriginal identity. There is no final acceptance of her predicament as it is seen in Glenyse Ward, although she herself uses it as a strategy to obtain the maximum response and empathy from the readers. Ruth Hegarty feels dislocated, dispossessed and displaced in the dormitory and she is aware of the fact that it is her Aboriginal identity that is responsible for her dormitory life. She conveys this forcefully in her book. She is also aware of the fact that she is deprived of motherhood as well as childhood as a dormitory girl/woman. This deprivation aggravates her sense of loss and dislocation.

Thus, it is the voice of a stolen child that is most striking in Ruth Hegarty's autobiography. Rather, it is an adult's voice recollecting her childhood, a child who is an Aboriginal, institutionalised, away from her society, parents, culture and liberty. Although Glenyse Ward is also located in the same context, consciousness of the situation and right indignation mark the autobiography of Ruth Hegarty, whereas acceptance and a seemingly passive response mark the autobiography of Glenyse Ward. And this contributes to the difference between the voices of Glenyse Ward and Ruth Hegarty, even though both of them speak as stolen and institutionalised Aboriginal dormitory children and domestics.

* * * * *

Although Sally Morgan says that working class consciousness dominates in *My Place*, it is in some of the other autobiographies that we find working class consciousness more dominant and poignant. For instance, Ruby Langford Ginibi's *Don't Take Your Love to Town* and Monica Clare's autobiographical novel *Karobran,* apart from Glenyse Ward's *Wandering Girl.* Sometimes this consciousness is marked by Aboriginal solidarity, and sometimes not. *Wandering Girl* has working class consciousness but that does not mean that Aboriginal consciousness is completely absent. She speaks as an Aboriginal domestic too. In the very first page of her autobiography, Glenyse Ward says:

> You see in the early days of survival and struggle, there was a lot of hardship and agony amongst the Aboriginal people. Through the misguided minds of the earnest white people we were taken away from our natural parents. This affected all of us. We lost our identity through being put into missions, forced to abide by the European way. (1987: 1)

But this consciousness does not turn into activism as it happens with some other Aboriginal writers, especially women writers. This autobiography or writer does not take the stand that personal is political though it/she consciously or unconsciously hints that to be born as an Aboriginal is political. It is not a battle to rescue the race but it is a struggle for her own release from the cage of discrimination based on race. On the other hand, though gender consciousness is not completely absent, as Glenyse Ward presents her experience of being a woman, the working class consciousness eclipses it.

Glenyse Ward discusses the issue of her Aboriginal identity as has been discussed earlier in this chapter. Although she discusses and comments on the Aboriginal situation and identifies herself as an Aboriginal girl, her working class consciousness comes to the fore. According to her; she is a black domestic. Irrespective of the racial differences, like Monica Clare in *Karobran,* Glenyse Ward makes friends with white men who belong to the working class and finds solace, encouragement and awareness in their company. She derives sufficient inspiration from a white worker to faintly protest against her white mistress. It is from him that she learns that her mistress has behaved badly even with the other maids who previously worked there.

The contribution of Monica Clare's *Karobran*, an autobiographical novel, to the working class consciousness cannot be ignored or denied. Although it is Isabelle's identity as a half-caste child that takes her away from her father and brother and orphans her at a very young age and makes her scramble about in search of her people and work, it is her working class consciousness that brings a realisation to her about the Aboriginal situation. She learns about the facts of working class life from the workers' meetings, becomes one of them, but feels the absence of Aboriginal people and Aboriginal voices in those meetings. She has many failures and frustrations in life as an Aboriginal girl who is in search of her people and of a livelihood. But it is the awareness and consciousness that she acquires in the company of workers and in the workers' union that turns her attention towards rural Aborigines and Aborigines in the reserves. Isabelle's identities as an Aborigine, as a woman and as a worker are intertwined. They are not distinct from each other, they are not isolated and unconnected. Her identity as an Aborigine directs her towards the working class; her identity as a woman imposes limitations on her livelihood; her Aboriginal woman's identity becomes a hurdle at every point of her working class life.

Thus the boundaries of race get thinner here for it is the working class consciousness which binds Monica Clare, like Glenyse Ward, to her Aboriginal maid's identity, and it binds her to her fellow workers, whether they are black or white. In both the books, we see a kind of acceptance of the predicament and also a protest against it. Glenyse Ward and Monica Clare go through the experience of domestics as well as independent workers and this contributes to their class-consciousness with racial issues integrated into it. The working class voice emerges dominant here, but that is the working class voice of the Aboriginal woman.

Another autobiography worth mentioning by an Aboriginal woman in which working class consciousness dominates is Ruby Langford Ginibi's *Don't Take Your Love to Town*. Her autobiography is her struggle to get ahead in life as a mother. She takes different kinds of jobs in order to be able to look after her children. Her identity is of an Aboriginal worker and her Aboriginal motherhood is what leads to this identity. Like Monica Clare, Ruby Langford Ginibi is also inspired by the workers' meetings and lectures. She shows concern for the Aboriginal issues, not only on the basis of race but also on the basis of class. In the case of Ruby Langford Ginibi race, class and gender all work together, which results in the working class Aboriginal woman's consciousness against the background of which the autobiography is set. She expresses solidarity with self-reliant Aboriginal women like her who had/have to shoulder comparable responsibilities. It is her constant search for work and shelter that characterises her autobiography. It is the story of a lower middle class or lower class Aboriginal woman for whom finding work is the main concern of life. Although race and gender matter very much in association with working class identity, it is this working class identity that decides the stability and standards of urban life. In her Acknowledgements, Ruby Langford Ginibi says,

> It is a true life story of an Aboriginal woman's struggle to raise a family of nine children in a society divided between black and white culture in Australia. . . . Dedicated also to every black

> woman who's battled to raise a family and kept her sense of humour. (1988: n.p.)

It is not merely a woman's story or an Aboriginal story. It is an Aboriginal woman's story. This Aboriginal woman has nine children dependent on her and she has to struggle to look after them for she does not have economic and familial security. In addition, she has to survive in a society which is racially divided and discriminating. It is here that Ruby Langford Ginibi's identity finds expression in multiple dimensions. Here is a poor, single Aboriginal mother of nine children, struggling for livelihood, struggling against discrimination, in search of social, economic and familial security. Although she does not achieve all these goals, her longing to achieve them makes her speak in different voices. Black, working class, poor, woman, urban, mother, independent, individual—all these are the multiple identities which encourage the multiple voices that articulate her concerns and commitments, agonies and anxieties. Her dedication of her autobiography to every black woman whose life is a battle hints that Ruby Langford Ginibi identifies herself with such women and is an evidence of her admiration for the traditional Aboriginal image of woman and her assumption of her identity. This in turn determines the voices in her autobiography.

Not only does Ruby Langford Ginibi discuss the issue of silence that prevails among Aboriginal people about women's business but she also reveals that she learnt in her childhood that there is a clear distinction between women's work and men's work, but not exploitation of the woman. This distinction according to her is a division of labour and responsibilities. Although her "eloped mother" always remains an oasis in her memories and provides solace to Ginibi amidst all kinds of hardships, she is not Ginibi's model in any sense. Only disappointments, desertions, frustrations and violence come Ginibi's way in her married life. As the title of her book reveals, she takes her love to town repeatedly with a hope for care, companionship, protection and familial security, but always in vain. In spite of this, she does not lose confidence in the institution of marriage or companionship. What she expects from this relationship is definitely not economic security, but a longing for the family and bonding, for she is self-reliant throughout her life. These are typical of Aboriginal life and it is these aspects of it that she dreams of and seeks. Not only does she look forward to a husband or a companion but also a father for her children and wishes that they should grow up safe and healthy within the institution of family. Here, her voice echoes the anxieties, dreams and aspirations of a lone woman, self-reliant, bold, capable, not aspiring for a "single life" but trying to pave the way to a "happy home."

When she longs for a man who would love her and shoulder the family responsibilities, Ginibi is not unaware of the fact that it is very difficult to find such a man. But the Aboriginal woman in her with a strong inclination towards "family" keeps her dreams and aspirations alive and fresh. The insecurity of employment and accommodation keeps her family always on the move, but she is never dispirited or shattered. It is not only this Aboriginal woman's perseverance that keeps her going, but also the determination of a mother that leads her in her repeated search for the ideal. In spite of surmounting difficulties, her motherhood is never adversely affected. When Ginibi repents of being a "permanent Eve," eating the apple and having babies, it is the mother in her who says, "I was the mother. I didn't know how to be not-mother" (1988: 202).

As a woman, her first priority is her children. Her consciousness of being a woman and her longing for familial bonds are, consequently, the crucial themes of her autobiography. Nor was everything smooth and easy for her in the process of asserting her identity as mother. She herself confesses: "though the association was wearing thin I tried to keep us together for the kids' sake. If he [her companion] was using me I was using him just as much. My first priority was the kids and it helped to have someone bringing in a wage now and then" (1988: 81). This statement reveals not only a woman's urge for a companion and a father for her children but also her working class needs for another earning hand in the family. This voice of Aboriginal woman/mother is strongly rooted in Aboriginal culture but violently dislocated and displaced from it.

Ruby Langford Ginibi, who gets only bashings and kicks from her husbands and companions, turns out to be sensitive to violence against women. It is the mother in her who retorts to her daughter's boyfriend beating up her daughter and it is the woman in her who questions him when her son beats up his girlfriend. Her motherhood thus extends itself as she gives shelter to the needy and adopts them, in spite of her own poverty and struggle for survival. The untimely death of some of her children provokes thought; the presence of her surviving children reminds her of who she is and what her future activity should be. This awareness leads her to a search for her roots and makes her aware of her nostalgia for Aboriginal culture, and ultimately paves the way for her writer-activist career. When Ginibi's son is waylaid and beaten up by a gang of white kids and her daughter is called "dirty abo," she faces this situation boldly. When she realises that in Australian jails, there are ten Aboriginal prisoners for each white prisoner and that many more blacks die in prison than whites, she gets motivated towards activism for Aboriginal issues.

This development of her personality and scope of activity is not only significant in the sense that Ginibi accommodates more people in her family as her children in spite of her poverty and insecurity, but also in the sense that at that time Aboriginal women, as many other Aboriginal women writers point out, had no rights over their children and were deprived of their motherhood. Against this background, where Aboriginal women had no control over their bodies, roles or relationships, where sexual atrocities, abortions, removal of children and the phenomenon of unwed Aboriginal mothers were an introduction to Aboriginal life, Ruby Langford Ginibi emerges successful as an Aboriginal woman. Although she is a failure as far as the material and romantic aspects of her life are concerned, she is successful as a truly contemporary Aboriginal woman. She asserts and reiterates her rights and responsibilities as a woman, as a mother and as an Aboriginal mother.

She subverts the power politics of the dominant society by deciding on the number of children that she can have, not only her own children, but adopted ones too. It is a triumph against the political, economic, social and cultural inflictions and indictments. She reinscribes the rights and capabilities of an Aboriginal woman in a colonised and institutionalised society, where she is not the coloniser but the colonised, not part of the institutionalising stratum but of the institutionalised. Thus she regains and retains the power of an

Aboriginal woman who believes in and works for preserving and protecting the institutions of marriage and family. When she speaks as a mother, it is most definitely the Aboriginal mother who is voicing her protest and her determination.

Ruby Langford Ginibi realises that her family is a microcosm of the Aboriginal situation in Australia. Readers also realise that Ginibi's experiences are not merely personal but can be extended to the condition of most Aboriginal women and children in a similar situation. The realisation about the question of colour dawns on her when she is taken to the mission—this seems to be the first step in the learning about the discriminating process of Aboriginal children. She says that the "black fellers" were identified and alienated everywhere, and in school, hospital and picture hall, there were separate seats for blacks and whites. While the Aboriginal children were given baths with handfuls of caustic soda used to wash linen instead of soap, they were not provided any medical care. Ginibi wonders if caustic soda was meant to change their black colour. Even if it was true, this colour does not fade but becomes a strong marker of identity and a factor in the segregation of Aboriginal people. This colour is not merely a biological fact but also a political factor. The fading of colour by assimilation is one of the major concerns of Aboriginal writers. Ginibi's detailed account of their baths with caustic soda works as a metaphor as well. Aboriginal people were considered dirty, unclean, black and ugly; they were bathed with caustic soda so that they may shed their "uncivilised" physical traits and habits. This in itself is a cruel imposition on the Aboriginal people. In spite of this imposition, they were not considered clean and civilised. As a metaphor, it also throws light, therefore, on the whole Aboriginal situation. Whites tried to "clear up" Aboriginal culture, languages and religion in order to "reform" and civilise the people, by imposing measures that the whites thought were perfect and apt. This behaviour is atrocious in itself, but in spite of having undergone it, Aboriginal people were not considered equal to the ruling whites.

Ruby Langford Ginibi recollects how as a child she was made conscious about her colour by the same treatment. She also speaks as a child who was not trusted in school and was asked to repeat tests to prove that she was not cheating. Perhaps this is what gives her confidence and a battling spirit in her later life, a perseverance to prove herself against all odds. She also speaks as a child who has always seen only white teachers but never black teachers. She contemplates, "Every teacher I'd ever seen was white. I tried to imagine black kids being taught by black teachers, then I tried to imagine white kids with black teachers" (1988: 37). This is the voice of a person who has never been trusted, who had to prove herself at every step. Probably this is what gives her the strength to move ahead.

It is very interesting that Ruby Langford Ginibi refers to "underprivileged children." She was herself deprived of privileges and remained underprivileged like many of her people. Although she is by no means underprivileged in intelligence and capability, she is underprivileged as a colonised girl in her constant poverty. When she refers to the experiences of children like her in the mission, it is the voice of the underprivileged that speaks. But, when she overtly refers to "underprivileged" children, there is no attempt on her part to identify with them though she does not seem to suggest that she is herself privileged.

If her colour consciousness in the mission teaches Ginibi that she is different from others, her next phase of colour consciousness begins when she joins Aunt Nell as an attendant when she goes there from the mission. Not only as a young Aboriginal attendant, but even after settling in a family in her own house, can Ginibi not escape from colour discrimination and humiliation. The group of Aboriginal families living in Green Valley, of which hers is one, is a butt of sarcastic comments from the white neighbourhood on the government's policy on integration. These are the families that are dislocated, alienated and who are isolated from their Aboriginal societies. In fact, it is not only alienation, but also a kind of imprisonment that it can be compared to the dormitory life. For even as grown ups the Aboriginal people are expected not to create noise or to disturb the white neighbourhood. It also reminds us of the reserves when Ginibi says that they could not entertain guests unless they had permission from the Commission. They live away from their Aboriginal surroundings, but remain Aboriginals in mind and identity. They escape from the clutches of missions and reserves in order to lead independent lives but still they have to go through a similar experience in the new state. Alienation, isolation, discrimination and restriction equally haunt them and torment them. Here, Ginibi's voice represents the voices of Aboriginal people who are restricted, belittled, silenced and dictated to. It reminds Ginibi of the mission. This lifestyle drastically affects her Aboriginal self. For in their Aboriginal existence, they often depended on being able to stay with friends and relatives. Whether they were inside a jail or outside, there was not much difference because both ways they were restricted and harassed.

These memories find a prominent place in Ruby Langford Ginibi's work. As an Aboriginal woman, she also writes about the common theme of the "belonging place." On her visit to her ancestral place, Bribie Island, she feels that the sun there returns her to life by soaking through her. She finds out how theories of human cultural development strategically prevent white students of culture, and Aborigines themselves, from acquiring respect for the latter. She wonders how her ancestors survived in Bribie Island. She feels proud to belong to such a tenacious race. She is also fascinated by the natural beauty and greatness of nature: "It made me think of our tribal beginnings, and this to me was like the beginning of our time and culture. Time was suddenly shortened to include all of history in the present, and it was also stretched to a way of seeing the earth that was thousands of years old" (Ginibi 1988: 234). Being culturally displaced, like other displaced persons, she simultaneously feels proud of her roots and nostalgia for them. This dilemma typifies contemporary Aboriginal culture in Australia. It is also what divides her voice into two. One speaks of her nostalgia and the other expresses her immense respect for and concern over the lost ancestors and cultural roots.

One of the subjects rather prominently unstudied in many Aboriginal women's autobiographies is that of atrocities against women within their own society. But in *When the Pelican Laughed* Alice Nannup does refer to Aboriginal practices, such as the attempts to "widow" her mother: "You see, it's law that when a woman's nyuba [partner] dies she's got to have all her hair cut off to make herself ugly for somebody else" (25). The same society that thrusts widowhood on an already deprived and grieving woman later forces her to marry another man. It is hardly a saving grace that the enforced widowhood is not "permanent." Both actions on the part of society clearly violate a woman's right to make such crucial decisions herself, it converts into mere custom what may very well be the turning points in individual life. Society thus not only restricts a woman's existence in the external world but also encroaches upon her inner world. It is, therefore, surprising that even after raising this subject Nannup does not voice a significant protest against such customs.

Rape is another phenomenon that defines atrocity against women the world over. It does figure in some works in the scope of this book. For instance, in *Mum Shirl* Shirley Smith does refer to this phenomenon in contemporary Australia. Whether it was an unusual or unheard of crime in indigenous society or not we may never know. But in contemporary society it seems to affect women. Aboriginal women are not infrequently raped. (Interestingly, on the other side, Aboriginal men are subject to accusations of raping white women.) Smith does indicate that rape of Aboriginal women is often brought on by the fact that they are Aboriginal, that it is induced by the cultural situation that has resulted from colonial subjugation of their societies. It is, therefore, one of the hazards of Aboriginal identity, as is the automatic suspicion that if a white woman has been raped, an Aboriginal man must have committed the crime.

Shirley Smith says, "Rape is another such crime that white people come down on the Black community for, even though through all the years very few Black men have raped white women and a great many white men have raped Black women" (33). She continues by saying that until recently it was unusual for an Aborigine to rape an Aboriginal woman or any other woman, for it is not the "Aboriginal way." She says that this threat of rape especially by white man instilled fear in Aboriginal girls. This holds a mirror up to the traditional Aboriginal societies and also to the predicament of Aboriginal men and women in a racially discriminating society. It is not just the question of culture conflict but also the issue of oppression and atrocities. Shirley Smith puts the centuries of white atrocities on Aboriginal women in a nutshell when she says that a great many white men have raped Black women and they have never been punished for that.

Shirley Smith's concern for Aboriginal women does not stop at the point of exposing their problems in a colonised society where their traditional roles are subverted. It also extends to the atrocities on Aboriginal women. She says that the Aboriginal identity is subjecting Aboriginal women to rape and Aboriginal men to accusation of rape in a white dominated society. Whether Shirley Smith discusses the condition of Aboriginal women in a cultural vacuum or the strength of their determination, it is the voice of an Aboriginal woman that speaks through her. It is the voice of an urban activist Aboriginal woman that speaks with a consciousness of her complex identity. It is full of concern for the violently displaced race exploited on the basis of gender as well.

Ruby Langford Ginibi quotes from Pam's speech which sounds like the shot guns aimed at the colonisers and their atrocities against indigenous people.

> It says a lot for what invasion has done to our people when we see our women suffering domestic violence, rape, incest, and problems of addiction. . . . Can you imagine what it's like for a Koori woman, raped and beaten, to have to go for help to the same organisations who stole her kids originally and the same lot who are killing her brothers—can you imagine how she feels about her so-called rights and protection? She knows she hasn't got any. (1994: 50)

Aileen Moreton-Robinson throws light also on the double bind of race and gender on Aboriginal women. She says that white men's assaults on indigenous women are attributed to indigenous women's promiscuity and their availability whereas indigenous men's sexual assaults on indigenous women are described as part of "murri love-making" by white male lawyers in court of law. In a similar tone, Payne argues that unlike white women, indigenous women are subject to three types of law: "white man's law, traditional law and bullshit law, the latter being used to describe a distortion of traditional law used as a justification for assault and rape of women" (10).

Such treatment of this and other subjects related to the sufferings of women is, however inadequate and infrequent in Aboriginal women's autobiographies. Sustained and critical treatment of indigenous violence and atrocities against women would have made the autobiographies of Aboriginal women even more important cultural and political statements. It would have provided a complex set of comparisons between indigenous and colonial atrocities, allowed us to distinguish between them, defined women's predicament better. If among the multiple voices heard in their autobiographies, some had been raised against *any* atrocity, our sympathy and understanding would have had a sharper edge. It is, on the other hand, not unlikely that such neglect is 'natural'—for virtually the whole attention of our writers seems focussed on colonially induced circumstances and experiences.

* * * * *

In her *Pride against Prejudice*, Ida West not only expresses her Aboriginal consciousness but also echoes the voice of a bold Aboriginal woman. Throughout, life is a battle for Aboriginal women in contemporary society; they have to fight their battle all alone. Whether they emerge triumphant or are defeated, it is their fighting spirit that is important for Aboriginal people, without which they cannot survive in their struggle for existence. Ida West says, "We had to fight our own battles. We got a hammering if we came home and said someone called us black. We stuck up for ourselves and weren't allowed to come home to tell tales. We had to get back in and fight" (22).

The problem of "half-castes" is another burning aspect of colonised Aboriginal life. Both Ruby Langford Ginibi and Shirley Smith express their concern and raise the issue in their autobiographies. Although most Aboriginal writers are half-castes, and consequently this becomes one of the major issues in their texts, it is in Ida West that the half-caste experience comes out most powerfully. Her Tasmanian childhood haunts her like it does in the case of many Aboriginal children. She does not go through the experiences of the stolen generation and dormitory life. But she has equally horrendous experiences in her childhood. That the whites considered Aboriginal people cannibals is one of the childhood memories that haunt Ida West. She understands and faces the fact even as a child that Aboriginal identity becomes a label and that everyone is born with a handle to her name. Discrimination in dance hall and church, her attempts to lighten her complexion with the help of powder and cream, whites talking to her in private but not in public—her childhood is marked by such memories. With all these experiences and memories, Ida West speaks in the voice of an Aboriginal woman, who attempted assimilation into white society with her lighter complexion, but who also realised that the boundaries and segregations were marked by strong discrimination and that she could be white in complexion but remains a half-caste in identity.

While Glenyse Ward narrates her unconscious actions of protest in her autobiography, Ida West narrates her conscious efforts at assimilation into white society. Glenyse Ward's unconscious efforts succeed but Ida West's conscious efforts go astray, for the discrimination is so strong that assimilation is impossible. Looking back at her past when she was a child, and her endeavours to become one with whites, Ida West not only comments on white discrimination but also on the futile assimilationist hopes of the blacks which had always been ultimately shattered. She describes what a tough struggle life has been for her, which reflects the Aboriginal consciousness of the writer and the relentless spirit of an Aboriginal woman, which is recurrently echoed in other Aboriginal women's autobiographies.

Ida West speaks in the voice of a half-caste who is neither accepted by whites nor admitted into their community by Aboriginals. Colour is the decisive factor in obtaining entry into either white or Aboriginal societies since racial identity is basically recognised on the basis of colour. Pamela Rajowski, in *Linden Girl: a story of outlawed lives* (1995), informs us that children of mixed blood were not highly valued in Aboriginal societies as full-blood children were. Full-blood children were perceived to have the right to be given knowledge of ancient beliefs, laws, traditions and customs. Aboriginal elders believed that a part Aboriginal child did not have the spiritual connections that a child with tribal parents had, and thus broke the family's line with their ancestral spirits. West is too light-skinned to get an entry into Aboriginal society. But she is not light-skinned enough for entry into white society as well. She remains an Aboriginal with her strong inclination towards Aboriginal life, culture and lineage, in spite of failure to be admitted into Aboriginal society. Anxiety for the loss of Aboriginal identity, culture and traits, predominant in most Aboriginal women writers, characterises Ida West's narrative as well:

> I think now and am proud of what we are and our talent . . . we are not afraid to think ourselves as good as the next one. It's been hard but we'll all get there. Some people think we don't know anything, probably we don't, but we still have feelings and love people, love our religion, our Saviour. We're not greedy, but I am afraid some of them will be before very much longer because they're learning greedy ways. . . . There is no love—no-one to give into people, no one to help one another in sickness. Money—you're no good without it, but you're no good with it. (54-55)

Alice Nannup, in her autobiography *When the Pelican Laughed*, states: "I never knew my grandfather, but his name was Sam Singh, and he was an Indian. . . . I'm Aboriginal, English and Indian—a real international person. You hear people run down the English but I never do, because that's a part of me, just like having Indian blood" (20). This statement reveals the writer's ready acceptance of the historicity of her identity as an Indian-Aboriginal-Australian woman. But what is her identity in the eyes of white Australian society? What is society's attitude towards her? Although the writer seems to be very clear about her identity in this statement, her autobiography does reveal her battle with society and in this battle her Aboriginal identity becomes the foundation, shield and weapon in different contexts.

It is not just colour, according to Alice Nannup's autobiography, which creates differences among Aborigines. As some of the interviews in Kevin Gilbert's *Living Black: Blacks Talk to Kein Gilbert* (1997) reveal, tribal identity and regional differences also play a very important role. For instance, let us examine two of Alice Nannup's statements:

> We were Nor'westers, see, we all stuck together. We loved one another, all the Northies always loved one another. We all belonged to one country, never mind if you're not related by blood, it's the North and that's our country. (120)

and

> we put the fire out because we could hear Aborigines a long way off and we were afraid. See, these were tribal people, and we didn't know what they'd do if they found us in their country. (144)

Nannup's statements throw light on her concept of identity and the way she differentiates herself from "other Aborigines" or the way she identifies "other Aborigines." This is a clear example of the fact that the Aborigines are not a "homogeneous group." In the recent self-conscious awareness-protest era, however, they have often tended to come together despite specific tribal identity and cultural difference.

Lionel Fogarty's poem "Identity" strengthens Alice Nannup's statements:

> In today's society the whites work on the divide and conquer
> One is to divide the identity to create the power.
> They have a full blood Aboriginal who says
> I know more about Aboriginal identity than an Aboriginal from the city.
> A half-caste will say
> I'm more intelligent than those full blood Aboriginals
> The blackfella whitefella say
> I'm more white than both of you put together. (Fogarty 33)

Thus Aboriginal women writers offer resistance in their autobiographies to the domination they suffer as women, as Aborigines and as Aboriginal women. The experience and expression that Jackie Huggins discusses in *Sister Girl* holds a mirror up to the consciousness that is expressed in the multiple and complex shift of voices of Aboriginal women writers in their autobiographies:

> As women we have all been subject to divide and rule socialisation, and racist and sexist ideologies. However, the overwhelming evidence and the experience of Aboriginal women points to the

> fact that Aboriginal women remain discriminated against due to their race rather than their gender. For example, a cosmetically apparent Aboriginal woman is regularly stereotyped on the basis of being a boong, coon, nigger, gin or abo far in excess of being a "woman." The lack of recognition and real understanding of this political difference is a major issue still to be resolved by the white women's movement. (1998: 25)

There are other kinds of consciousness and voices that emanate from and prevail in these autobiographies. For instance, Christian consciousness/identity and westernised lifestyle. These will be discussed in the next chapter "Conflicting Identities." These identities come into conflict with indigenous identities of the writers whereas in the case of voices discussed in the present chapter, with all their differences, they contribute to the harmony among the writer's voices.

Conflicting Identities

Ruby Langford provides a key to the contemporary Aboriginal situation when she says, "everything pertaining to us Abos has always been political, ever since Cook landed here" (Ginibi 1994: 42). Knowing that being born Aboriginal is being political, Aboriginal women's autobiographies become books of instruction for readers in decolonising history and articulating an Aboriginal version of it. The existing Aboriginal identity constructed by the whites gets blurred and an Aboriginal identity from an Aboriginal perspective is created in these autobiographies. Literature about Aborigines, for the first time, also becomes subjective here after being released from the clutches of "objective" presentation of Aborigines by the whites. Thus the political and subjective strands mark the books chosen for analysis in this book.

As these Aboriginal women writers try to reconstruct their identity, to escape from the identity constructed by the other, the conflicting strands in the identities of the writers come to the forefront. It is not easy to differentiate the reconstruction clearly from the already constructed identity. The point where these two overlap becomes the point of difficulty for the writers to pronounce their stand without ambiguity, hesitation and vacillation. Even if they succeed in doing so, the reader also faces the same problems, whether to go by the writer's or by the mainstream society's or by her own judgement. This leads to the conflict of identity or the conflicting identities of the writer. This chapter will discuss the above issue in the light of different aspects of Aboriginal women's autobiographies.

Sally Morgan's *My Place* presents the writer's desperate longing to reach out to her roots. Her grandmother Gladys represents the Aboriginal women of the previous generations. She has neither lost the physical traits nor acquired Aboriginal skills. Black in complexion, non-white in features, Sally Morgan says that her grandmother has immense love for nature and animals; she identifies and sympathises with all Aborigines, believes in Aboriginal medicine, religion and practices. Like an indigenous woman violently placed in an alien culture and looked down upon by "civilisation," she is scared of hunger, natural calamities, discrimination and the police. She lives every minute dreading threats from these. Ironically, she loves her Aboriginal identity but at the same time desperately tries to hide it.

Sally Morgan's mother is another symbol of Aboriginal consciousness:

> Mum was passionately interested in the world of nature, and avidly watched any television programme dealing with cruelty to animals. She would sit in her favourite chair by the fireside and, between sobs, decry the brutality of man. . . . Her passion was for the dead as well as the living. (Morgan 90)

The principle of life for people who live in association with nature anywhere in the world is awareness of nature. This awareness becomes the code of life for them because they depend on nature for their survival and sustenance and look upon nature as a gift given to them. From this follows a special respect for nature. This in turn leads to their concept of caretakership of and responsibility towards nature. Since they live in close association and partnership with nature, they also learn how to face and escape from dangers. The second stage of awareness is concern for it. Whether it is thought of as Mother Earth or Mother Nature, its worship is a result of awe and responsibility towards nature.[1] Similar is the case of the Aboriginal people of Australia. Since even their central creation myth is essentially naturalistic, we can conclude that this concern characterises traditional Aboriginal existence. (It is unlikely to be otherwise in other pre-technological communities around the world. At the same time, it is also likely to be different from a deep interest in nature that is protectively missionary or objectively scientific that characterises some people in the modern world.) Let us consider the birth of "First Woman" in the Australian Aboriginal Creation Myth "The First Man." The yacca tree's flower stalk grew rounder, limbs began to form from it and "with a shock Man realised that the tree was changing into a two-legged creature like himself" (Reed 1998: 18). That is how woman takes birth more or less directly from nature, thus suggesting that nature and the human being are one. There are also other stories among the myths, some of which have been discussed in the Introduction before this. They depict the change of humans into animals, trees, rocks and streams. This is a clear indication of erasing the barriers between human life and nature and establishing interaction and bond between them.

This "love" of nature is actually a serious awareness and concern, both of which characterise Aboriginal life, according to Sally Morgan in her autobiography. For example, Sally Morgan's mother retains her Aboriginal consciousness though she no longer has an unalloyed or a complete Aboriginal appearance. Nor does she openly admit her Aboriginal identity. She does not reveal her and her family's Aboriginality to her children and when her mother tells her grandchildren that they are Indians, Sally Morgan's mother does not question the statement. This reticence may be traced to her marriage to a white man. Sally Morgan herself expresses her belief in Aboriginal customs and practices. She understands the birdcall heard before her grandmother's death. She feels the presence of the spirits of her ancestors. Throughout the autobiography she conforms to her Aboriginal consciousness and reasserts her Aboriginality, though she herself lives away from Aboriginal culture and is not really aware in specific terms of her Aboriginal lineage.

Like Aboriginality, Aboriginal consciousness is also a term which can be interpreted in multiple ways. It is not a single, essential quality that defines Aboriginality. In trying to define Aboriginal consciousness, there is a danger of falling into theorising a lifestyle and imprisoning it in the framework of jargon. Since the models that we have before us are all, starting from the use of the word Aborigine, given by the colonisers, it also becomes difficult to define and interpret such concepts from within the Aboriginal ethos. Yet the use of western or colonial terms is unavoidable. When we refer to a society or community living in close association with nature or in dependence on nature, it does not in any way mean that only tribal societies live in association with nature and not any other societies. All living beings depend on nature for their survival and sustenance. But the kind of tribal societies which the Australian Aboriginal communities represent, as Aboriginal oral and written literatures unveil, have immense respect for nature and strive towards harmony between nature and human beings. Before the colonial life-style, they kept the food chain going and thus achieved ecological balance, for they neither killed nor destroyed more than they needed. Land was essential part of their being and lifestyle. They believed in the sacredness of the land that is their spirituality (Ginibi 1994). Thus their belief, lifestyle and knowledge imbibe respect and concern for nature and other living beings. When it is said that in part Aboriginal consciousness may be defined as love for nature it is not in the tone of calling Aboriginal people savages or primitives or projecting them as exotic people. One is, however, definitely setting them apart from self-conscious modern associations and organisations working towards protection of nature and environment.

This sense of Aboriginality, which they inherit as part of cultural transmission and which establishes sense of belonging or oneness, also means resistance to western lifestyle in a way, since the principles that guide Aboriginal life and western life contradict each other. We can draw this conclusion from Aboriginal literature. The historical fact of their inability today to retreat into their original relationship with nature also makes them nostalgic about this loss. Anne Brewster rightly observes that many Aboriginal people see their spirituality as an emblem of Aboriginality. While discussing Aboriginal spirituality in *My Place*, Brewster says that here it takes various forms and that one of these is a love of the bush. The swamp and the bush also instill in the children a love of nature and become a part of their consciousness: "From this point of view it has a spiritual significance and is a site of comfort and protection" (Brewster 1996: 27). This sense, in other words, participates in consciousness of the colonial situation. In Alan Lawson's words, post-colonialism is a "politically motivated historical-analytical movement [which] engages with, resists, and seeks to dismantle the effects of colonialism in the material, historical, cultural-political, pedagogical, discursive, and textual domains" (156). In the current

Aboriginal situation, it is not merely the effects of the past colonisation but also the ongoing colonisation within which the discourse of the writers takes place, and in this postcolonial consciousness, awareness of past relationship with nature figures prominently.

For instance, Sally Morgan and her grandmother speak out against hospitals, in the process providing for a critique of the wider white society which the hospitals represent. The western approach to life is repeatedly criticised because it fails to understand life in its fullness. The contrast between western materialistic approach and Aboriginal spiritual approach to the complex totality of human experience is firmly established in several women's autobiographies. Although written in part in a western mode and the coloniser's language, one can see degrees of postcolonial awareness in *My Place,* as in other Aboriginal texts, in its hankering after indigenous life in order to oppose the colonisers' culture. Anita Heiss observes,

> In terms of defining Aboriginal writing as "post-colonial" literature, it appears that there are two distinct views. First, that of the literary establishment who use the term as a way of describing a genre in which Aboriginal people write; and second, that of most Aboriginal writers who see the term implying that colonialism is a matter of the past and that decolonisation has taken place, which of course is not the case. (Ruffo 226)

In connection with this last idea, the questions that Kathryn Trees and Colin Johnson raise about the term postcolonial are interesting: does the postcolonial suggest colonialism is quite over? They say that postcolonialism is a "white" concept and that definitely it is not only colonialism for Aboriginal people in the past, because internal racial discrimination continues in Australia (Trees and Johnson 264-65). In contrast, Melissa Lucashenko agrees that their writing reflects the effects of being colonised. Lucashenko says that everything in her life, including her writing, is touched by or has risen out of colonialism, not being able to grow out of anything traditional. She says, "I'm not saying that we're not oppressed, I'm saying that what I define as a colonial era is ending and now the oppression is still there, but the circumstances of our oppression are changing" (Ruffo 228).

Anne Brewster emphasises that postcolonialism does not apply to the Aboriginal situation. She refers to various definitions of postcolonialism, one of which is Gayatri Chakravorty Spivak's analysis that postcolonialism assumes that decolonisation has taken place (Spivak 65-76). Brewster says, "Aboriginal people do not produce narratives of postcoloniality or even decolonisation, although in their demand for self-determination they certainly articulate what Ngugi (1986) calls 'decolonising the mind'. What they write and speak are narratives of continuing dispossession and surveillance" (1995: 20). The definition of postcolonialism given by Alan Lawson mentioned earlier seems to be quite relevant to the voices raised by Aboriginal women writers. This is exactly what we find in Australian Aboriginal women's autobiographies in general and in Sally Morgan's *My Place* in particular.

It has been suggested here that the Aboriginal consciousness of man's place in nature is not merely a matter of mythology or the recent resurgence in exotic-looking tribal art, or a mere creation of cultural reconstruction. For the contention that these three themes are essentially related in the writing of at least the Aboriginal women, can be adduced in support some passages from the autobiographies. These examples will show the link that was proposed among concern for nature, Aboriginal consciousness and identity, and postcoloniality or awareness of existence in a postcolonial situation. In her story of God's gift to his very few special people, Marnie Kennedy says that God said,

> I have chosen to give *this land* and all *its riches* to the black race, a race of people who will *not destroy its natural beauty*. They will *live in harmony with all that is given them*. They *will be made aware of the dangers* of wild animals and reptiles and of the sea that will surround them. They *will have their own healing ways from the things given them*. . . . This land will be their paradise and *these people will remain humble and proud and will worship none other than the beauty that is theirs*. (61; my italics)

In Ida West's *Pride against Prejudice*, we find examples such as the following, very practical yet sympathetic or harmonious, description:

> We did our share of black tracking. If we were out in the bush, we would make signs to get home. We could track down snakes. We could tell which way the snakes were going on the soft sand.
>
> We learned to tell if the snake was going away or towards the house. A snake never liked to travel over buffalo grass—they would go over it slowly, as they couldn't cling to the leaves. (25)

In *When the Pelican Laughed*, Nannup makes explicit the claim that it is a long-standing tradition:

> There are pools all over that country and you're not allowed to go near them unless you make your peace, that's the Aboriginal law. As soon as you do that, and you're accepted, you can have a drink. But if you don't do it, and just take from the pool, then anything can happen to you. That's beautiful isn't it? *To keep your tradition and never let it go.* (224, my italics)

Margaret Tucker goes a step farther, in *If Everyone Cared* to an influential instance in her life of how her mother treated creatures:

> Sometimes Mother got up at night to attend to animals whimpering with the cold, to make them comfortable in a corner on an old bag or something. I saw her once help a beautiful, proud, fierce-looking eagle that a gun-happy youth had shot down, breaking its wing. I don't know how she fixed up the wing, but she kept the fire burning to keep it warm. There was a huge goanna too, that was wounded with a pea rifle. She taught us compassion for hurt things, and especially for hurt people. (64-65)

And finally, Noonuccal states in so many words the ultimate instructions related to this harmonious and responsible relationship of man and nature: "One rule he [her father] told us we must strictly obey. When we went hunting, we must understand that our weapons were to be used only for the gathering of food. We must never use them for the sake of killing. This is in fact one of the strictest laws of the Aborigine, and no excuse is accepted for abusing it" (1972: 6). Instances of this kind of proof, of the way Australian Aboriginal people were expected to live in the midst of the riches of nature, can be easily multipled.[2]

Another crucial factor in their assertion of identity is their pride in their Aboriginality. They do not express any self-pity for their present condition, rather a nostalgia for their Aboriginal past and a protest against present discrimination. Although they are treated as inferiors by the white society at every step, Aboriginal women writers do not give up their battle. For example, Ida West declares:

> We were always brought up by our mother and father to think of ourselves as good as the next one. We came into the world head first and we go out feet first, and that goes for everybody, without the breech baby. So Europeans are made no better, and they smell just the same when they pass away, so there is no difference. God made us all—as long as we get by and try to help people and not be so greedy by wanting everything. (8)

These words may work not only as eye openers for white readers but also encourage the Aborigines to release themselves from the prejudiced and inhibited notions that prevail in society. This attitude reveals not only the Aboriginal concept of fraternity and equality but also attacks the rigidly stratified western society. True, Ida West is encouraged to consider herself equal to whites. But do whites consider her their equal? Their opinion may not matter to her as a postcolonial protesting individual and also because her autobiography is a protest against whites. But the possibility of a different reaction to Ida West's assertion of identity may lead once again towards an identity crisis.

Sally Morgan's grandmother expresses her agony saying, "You know, Sal . . . all my life, I been treated rotten, real rotten. . . . I been treated like a beast. Just like a beast of the field. And now, here I am . . . old. Just a dirty old blackfella" (352). This statement mirrors the fears and reasons of Sally Morgan's grandmother and the reasons behind her attempts to hide her Aboriginality. When she says that she has been treated like a beast, she is voicing the agony of all Aborigines who have been treated like beasts. The word beast echoes with multiple meanings and the ways in which she was understood and treated by the whites. A beast is, first of all, not a human being like the whites. A beast is uncivilised, fit for hard toil only, and it can be owned or disowned and disposed of. When she says that she is just a dirty old blackfella, she expresses the white people's contempt for blacks. For Aborigines, their fellow Aborigines are blackfellas. But for whites, all Aborigines are dirty blackfellas. This statement of Sally's grandmother discloses her disgust with her past, contempt for her present and fear for her future or rather for her family's future.

This issue of the Aborigines' effort to hide their identity is not much emphasised in other autobiographies. The main reason for this seems to be that apart from narrating her own story, Sally Morgan makes her people narrate their family history as well. Other narrators are given as much importance as Sally Morgan enjoys in her autobiography, perhaps even more. This does not happen in other autobiographies, though other writers too make an effort to narrate Aboriginal stories while narrating their own story. Moreover, the changing attitude of the contemporary generation towards their Aboriginal identity may also be responsible for this. Sally Morgan's grandmother is scared of her identity because of her suffering in life and tries to hide her identity. At the same time she cannot deny it either. Contrary to this, Sally Morgan accepts, declares, constructs and asserts her Aboriginal identity. This does not merely represent an attitudinal change in a family but a change in the political situation of Aborigines in Australia.

As the readers go through *My Place* and try to understand Sally Morgan's struggle to come to terms with her Aboriginal identity, some inevitable questions do confront them: How did Sally Morgan come to terms with her "Indian identity"? Did she try to search for "Indian roots" as she did with her Aboriginal identity? Between her being told that she is an Indian and her finding out that her lineage is in fact Aboriginal, not much is said about her feelings and experiences as an "Indian." This particular phase of Sally Morgan's life remains completely undiscussed. Is the exclusion of everything other than Aboriginal deliberate? As an "Indian," what were her experiences and her reactions to those experiences? Why does this phase remain unrepresented?

Another dimension of this crucial concept of identity is the Aboriginal dilemma about Aboriginality. Aboriginality is defined in a number of ways that sometimes radically differ from each other. The concept of Aboriginality according to the Aborigines may be different from that of whites. Ross Watson, an activist, says in *Living Black,*

> But what is Aboriginality? Is it being tribal? Who is an Aboriginal? Is he or she someone who feels that the Aboriginals are somehow dirty, lazy, drunken, bludging? Is an Aboriginal anyone who has some degree of Aboriginal blood in his or her veins and has demonstrably been disadvantaged by that? Or is an Aboriginal someone who has had the reserve experience? Is Aboriginality institutionalised gutlessness, an acceptance of the label "the most powerless people on earth"? Or is Aboriginality, when all the definitions have been exhausted, a yearning for a different way of being, a wholeness that was presumed to have existed before 1776? (Gilbert 1978: 184)

Apart from stating that Aboriginality depends on several aspects of life, these questions and debates also push writers into a dilemma as to whether they can be called Aborigines or not and whether they are entitled to the benefits of Aboriginal identity which they claim in their autobiographies.

Jackie Huggins, on the other hand, makes it clear that whatever may be her definition of Aboriginality, she does not agree with the white assumption of Aboriginality. She says,

> Foremostly, I detest the imposition that anyone who is non-Aboriginal can define my Aboriginality for me and my race. Neither do I accept any definition of Aboriginality by non-Aboriginals as it insults my intelligence, spirit and soul, and negates my heritage. (1993: 459)

While the above two statements present the individual stands on behalf of their community about Aboriginality, Sally Morgan expresses her dilemma about her Aboriginality:

> Had I been dishonest with myself? What did it really mean to be Aboriginal? I'd never lived off the land and been a hunter and a gatherer. I'd never participated in corroborees or heard stories of the Dreamtime. I'd lived all my life in suburbia and told everyone I was Indian. I hardly knew any Aboriginal people. What did it mean for some one like me? (141)

This debate or such questions are really crucial in Aboriginal autobiographies. Is it possible for anybody to claim Aboriginality without experiencing the Aboriginal predicament? What decides Aboriginality: awareness, experience, expression, sympathy, empathy, activism or lineage? In contemporary Australia, does Aboriginality mean being a hunter and gatherer, participating in corroborees and hearing Dreamtime stories and growing with an Aboriginal identity? Or is it staying away from all these things, but at the same time longing for them, unaware of or even trying to escape from Aboriginal identity? What is the nearest description of Aboriginality or Aboriginal identity or Aboriginal situation in contemporary Australia? Whichever comes close to reality for each person must be the real definition of any concept. That way, Sally Morgan, in expressing her doubts about her Aboriginality, also asserts her right to claim Aboriginality. This is not ambiguity or paradox, but the reality of those robbed of their heritage.

Not only does she assert her Aboriginal identity, but she also tries to define it. Her statement reveals that according to her, Aboriginality is living off the land, living like a hunter and gatherer, participating in corroborees and listening stories of the Dreamtime. Does this really reflect the Aboriginal consciousness of contemporary times? When Australia was uninvaded and Aboriginal life was uninterfered with, Sally Morgan's definition or understanding of Aboriginality may have been apt. But, given the facts of colonisation, urbanisation, and discrimination, the Aboriginal experience amounts to a diversion from "Aboriginal lifestyle."

It has already been mentioned that Sally Morgan asserts her indigenous roots like all other Aboriginal writers. That most Aboriginal writers are part-Aboriginals or part-whites is an undeniable fact. This affords them a clear insight into the problems of Aborigines in the process of acculturation. This also equips them to express anxiety about the gradually disappearing Aboriginal traits and qualities and Aboriginal lifestyle. A very strong Aboriginal consciousness and a compulsion to hide their Aboriginal identity and to lose their physical traits that stand for the Aboriginal lineage lead to the conflict within themselves and also between them and white society. Their physical traits lost, traditional lifestyle and location lost—then what Aboriginal identity remains with them, except their Aboriginal consciousness? Once again, to quote Sally Morgan:

> I suppose, in hundreds of years' time, there won't be any black Aboriginals left. Our colour dies out; as we mix with other races, we'll lose some of the physical characteristics that distinguish us now. I like to think that, no matter what we become, our spiritual tie with the land and the other unique qualities we possess will somehow weave their way through to future generations of Australians. I mean, this is our land, after all, surely we've got something to offer. (306)

Aboriginal writers mostly refer to the Aboriginal loss of land, language, culture and liberty. This is one place where Sally Morgan expresses her concern for the loss of physical traits that stand for Aboriginality. This is another crucial deciding factor, for Aboriginal identity which perversely becomes the basis of their colour and features in a white dominated society. Although black colour is despised and Aboriginal physical features are ridiculed by the whites and discrimination occurs on the basis of their physical traits, Sally Morgan expresses concern for their loss. She does not express happiness about acculturation, which results in the loss of Aboriginal qualities. She says that unfortunately acculturation is resulting in the loss of their Aboriginal lineage. Aboriginal literature fights for equality and at the same time, as it is articulated in the above quotation, it also fights for retaining and preserving their Aboriginal identity and continued existence. Sally Morgan's words succeed in expressing anguish for the eliminated Aboriginality and in reasserting the Aboriginal identity and attachment to Aboriginal culture and land. The identity crisis emanates from the conflict between Aboriginal consciousness and a longing for Aboriginal lifestyle and the loss of physical traits of Aboriginal people.

Ruby Langford Ginibi also expresses similar concern for the disappearing Aboriginality and strongly attacks the isolationist policies of the government. Although they have their own homes only in name, the Aborigines are chained and imprisoned in restrictions imposed by the government and the discriminatory attitude of society. She says,

> The government policy of assimilation by absorption meant splitting up the Aboriginal communities, and I understand what this policy meant as I had four daughters and only one married an Aboriginal. My grandchildren are blond and blue or hazel-eyed, and within two or three hundred years there won't be Aboriginals in suburbia. So far as the government is concerned, assimilation by absorption is working well, and in the end, there'll be no Aboriginal problem whatever. (Ginibi 1988: 176-77)

This is another context in which this concern for Aboriginal identity is strongly expressed. Assimilation by absorption may result only in the elimination of Aborigines. After some time there will be only part-Aborigines who the government thinks can be reformed since they have white blood in them. Thus there will be no more Aboriginal problems because there will be no Aborigines at all. On the one hand, white society's efforts to destroy Aboriginal identity and on the other Aborigines' endeavour to protest and preserve their Aboriginality—these two forces engender the conflicting identities of Aborigines. In spite of such apparently insurmountable hurdles, this conflict results in a more powerful assertion of Aboriginal identity and in an increasingly intense struggle to champion the identity that has been tampered with by discrimination and assimilation.

Aboriginal religions and Christianity are two vastly different ways of life and Australian Aborigines have, with all their spiritual traditions, inevitably had to embrace Christianity. There are some writers who reveal their immense devotion to Christ. But there are also writers who come down heavily on the side of Aboriginal religion. Ida West, however, proposes a sort of harmony between Aboriginal religion and Christianity. Her parents belonged to these two different religions and their children believed in and practised both religions. She refers to this fact in her autobiography. Yet, simultaneously, her memory may have forced her to reveal some bitter aspects of her religious life, for instance, that as a child she and her siblings were forcibly taken to church and were ordered to follow the proceedings and observe the rites. These two parts of her testimony clash with each other and raise doubts as to whether the reason behind her reluctance in going to the church was her childishness or her dislike of Christianity. Here is the confused religious identity of Ida West, who confesses in her autobiography that she and her family members were all devout Christians, yet she also records that she was taken to church forcibly. She was a Christian by overt religious identity, yet she remained an Aboriginal Christian and this fact has obviously influenced her religious life.

We also come across another instance of a devout Aboriginal Christian in Aboriginal women's autobiographies. Glenyse Ward, in her autobiography *Wandering Girl,* accepts Christianity and the image of nuns as sources of succour and this forms a crucial feature of her autobiography. Brought up in a Catholic mission, Glenyse Ward remains a faithful follower of Christianity but her love of nature and living beings, which is a fundamental principle of Aboriginal religion, guides her throughout her life. Her Christian identity does not trouble her at all. She happily admits that identity and she wants to remain a Christian, for that matter she never debates her religious identity. It is the church that looked after her as a child and it is the church that provides her livelihood. But what kind of life and livelihood the church has given her and what the influence of the church is on her, are important questions. It is true that she grew up in a Catholic mission but she also grew up as an Aboriginal girl. Similarly, the Church provides her employment but as a virtual slave in a white household. She is taught in the Catholic mission not to talk unless she is spoken to and never to talk back. She has had to imbibe the idea of white superiority during her stay in the fold of the church that moulds her into a good slave. Thus, there may not be an overt conflict between her Aboriginal religious identity and her Christian identity, for Ward does not know or remember much about her Aboriginal religion. Clearly, Glenyse Ward's Aboriginal identity has been subjugated in the name of religion and welfare. The Christianity that Glenyse Ward was forced to embrace teaches her only to degrade her Aboriginal identity. Therefore, although there is no conflict in her mind about her religious identity, her Christian identity definitely affects and moulds her Aboriginal identity in an adverse manner and this almost directly leads to the conflict her Aboriginal identity has to face in the white dominated society. In her autobiography *Don't Take Your Love to Town*, Ruby Langford Ginibi states that western religion cannot encompass life in its fullness, whereas Aboriginal religion definitely does so. But there is no direct criticism of Christ and Christianity and the writer herself seems to be a believing Christian like most other Aborigines and Aboriginal writers.

It is in Sally Morgan's *My Place* that we come across a direct attack on the principles of Christianity:

> Take the white people in Australia, they brought the religion here with them and the Commandment, Thou Shalt Not Steal, and yet they stole this country. They took it from the innocent. You see, they twisted the religion. That's not the way it's supposed to be. (213)

At least some Aborigines think that it was not the religion but the white people that twisted them. And they also know that Christians were not supposed to indulge in such outrageous contradiction of their religion. The Aboriginal people realised, sooner or later, that white people stole their land, using religion as a weapon, even though their own religion strictly prohibited stealing. Once again it is not Christ and Christianity that are attacked but the attitude of white "Christians." Sally Morgan's granduncle Arthur, who speaks the above words, expresses his invincible faith in the Christian concept of God.

A similar instance of a devout Christian protesting against the way in which whites practise Christianity may be seen in Shirley Smith's autobiography *Mum Shirl.* Shirley Smith admits that hers was a Roman Catholic family and that her mother was called "Mad Roman Catholic" by non-believers. Shirley Smith also reveals that she enjoyed her mother being referred to like that because there was respect in it. But she also says that she rebelled against the priest who overlooked her because of her Aboriginal identity. She, indeed, walked out of the church after an argument with the priest and kept away for almost fifteen years:

> Catholics say one thing and do another. They talk about all people being equal and all being God's children, and they then go about treating Aboriginal people as though they had no rights, or as though they didn't exist. The Catholic churches, too, are built upon

> land that has been stolen from Aboriginal people, and that doesn't seem to bother the Catholics at all. (Shirley Smith 37)

This seems to reveal trust in Christian principles but not in Christian practice. Mum Shirl, in her autobiography, protests vehemently against the practice. The distance between the preaching and the practice of Christian people is strongly criticised by Mum Shirl, because it was one of the factors that determined the predicament of Aborigines. Equality and rights, and injunctions against crimes like stealing were never put into practice by whites; moreover, they were used against the Aborigines by luring them with a religion like Christianity. That the churches were built on Aboriginal land stolen by whites itself puts the principles and practice of Christianity by whites into question.

This strong belief in Aboriginal religion and questioning of Christian practice from an Aboriginal perspective have led to an identity crisis. It has become one of the themes of Aboriginal literature, especially Aboriginal women's autobiographies. This crisis raises several questions in the readers. For instance, are these writers, spiritually, Christians or Aborigines? Are they both? If they are both, is it possible to achieve such harmony between two religions? If they are neither, why and how do they carry the double burden of religious identity? In her interview with Delys Bird and Dennis Haskell, when asked about her conflict between Christianity and Aboriginality, Sally Morgan says:

> I think there is a conflict when people make it a conflict, you know, but also people are amazingly flexible. Spirituality doesn't function on one level, it functions in layers, and so you might have a form of spirituality in the Christian sense but then you can have another from outside of that which is just as valuable, and that tends to be what happens in Aboriginal people. They will function on one level and you will talk about certain things in certain ways within a Christian context. If you happen to be a church goer, when you are outside that formalised institution you can function on another level of spirituality which you then talk about. There are some things that you only share with certain people. I think that people can function on lots of different levels without there being a conflict. (Bird and Haskell 11-12)

It is amazing to hear from Sally Morgan that conflict arises when people *make* it a conflict. Her own autobiography is full of conflict. A constant debate goes on between her sense of Aboriginal religion and her Christianity and this conflict comes out in the book subtly but definitely. When she says that people can function at different levels without there being a conflict, she does not, surprisingly, refer to the conflict such a situation can engender. In any case, clearly, one would have to face some conflict if one is forced to or wants to function at different levels. Especially in a country like Australia where every part of Aboriginal life has been colonised, it cannot be easy to live without a spiritual or religious conflict. When Christianity is superimposed on Aboriginal religions or Aboriginal religions are replaced by Christianity, both of which phenomena have happened in Australia, there is bound to be conflict. Especially when there is force and compulsion, it is all the more difficult. This must, surely lead to conflict of religious identities. And such crises have formed a crucial part of the identity crisis among the Aborigines, especially Aboriginal women. For as women they would be subjected to or exposed to many more kinds of conflicts in different aspects of life from different angles.

In connection with religion and spirituality, we cannot but glance at the ritualistic Aboriginal societies and the role of women. Diane Bell's *Daughters of the Dreaming* helps us with a brilliant picture of Aboriginal women and their role in and attachment to rituals. She says,

> What I saw was a strong, articulate and knowledgeable group of women who were substantially independent of their menfolk in economic and ritual terms. Their lives were not ones of drudgery, deprivation, humiliation and exploitation because of their lack of penis and attendant phallic culture, nor was their self-image and identity bound up solely with their child-bearing and child-rearing functions. Instead I found the women to be extremely serious in the upholding, observance and transmission of their religious heritage. Religion permeated every aspect of their lives. (Bell 231)

What happens to these strong, articulate and knowledgeable women in contemporary male-dominated white society? Going by Diane

Bell's words, what happens to the all-pervading religion in their lives in a society where spirituality and religion are defined in a very different manner? If religion and rituals play such a crucial role in an Aboriginal woman's life, has not a void been created in her mind and life without rituals? Is it as easy as Sally Morgan says to state that there is no conflict? Does the changing role of Aboriginal woman in her transition from bush to settlement life not create any conflict in Aboriginal women's lives? We come across Aboriginal women in Aboriginal literature who emphasise that it was the arrival of missionary presence which created shame, as it was the institutionalisation of settlement life which created households in which women were dependants. Their lives had not been full of drudgery, deprivation, humiliation and exploitation in Aboriginal societies. How did they adjust to the completely different society outside? Even if they live with black men, what is their predicament in the changed atmosphere and changing frustrated companionship? What happens in Aboriginal societies is as important as what happens in the urban situation of Aboriginal women. What is their position in urban society? The image that Diane Bell depicts comes alive in Aboriginal women's autobiographies and also raises questions. Diane Bell continues:

> I am suggesting it as not only the opportunities available to Aboriginal women but also the white perception of woman's role which constrained Aboriginal women. Missionaries needed to create God-fearing women who knew shame. In addition white bosses needed women to perform a number of duties and to fulfil a number of roles. Cattle station managers wanted workers who were all-round helpers. Of course in frontier conditions the usual double standards applied to women, who were expected to work hard during the day and to please the master in the evenings. Women on missions did not escape sexual exploitation either. (96)

When women are exploited at so many levels and in so many ways, there is bound to be conflict in their mind and society about their identity and their roles. Diane Bell says that not only white men harmed Aboriginal women but also the white woman too helped in destroying the image and status of woman from an Aboriginal perspective. The contemporary situation reasserts this kind of exploitation, provides more avenues of exploitation having been created for Aboriginal women. This contemporary woman who is neither black nor white, who cannot identify with blacks and will not be received by whites, suffocates between the identities that have only victimised her in a society where gender is an extra burden for individuals of the already suffering marginalised sections. This conflict is undoubtedly reflected in Aboriginal women's autobiographies.

Keeping in mind the limitations of Diane Bell as a researcher, that she was an outsider however honest and thorough she was in her research and the fact that the field of her research was not a natural habitat but a government colony, we may be able to consider her statements only with a degree of scepticism. But the issue of the silence and secrecy that Aboriginal women practise especially in spiritual matters appeals to her readers. The conflicting identities of an Aboriginal woman—as a traditional Aboriginal woman with Aboriginal heritage and an Aboriginal woman in a coloniser's society—leads to several strategies adopted by Aboriginal women writers in exposing the white atrocities, one among which is silence. Silence is the most powerful weapon if it is effectively and rightly used. The same thing happens here. Not only presence but absence also can "speak" volumes when it is employed at crucial junctures and this is one of the features we definitely see in Aboriginal autobiographies.

* * * * *

Similar conflicting identities arise when these writers discuss the question of matriarchy and feminism. For instance, Sally Morgan, like in her other statements, proves to be controversial even when she talks about matriarchy in her family. In her interview with Mary Wright, "A Fundamental Question of Identity," she says: "It's a matriarchal society. . . . I know I'm domineering! And Mum is in her way, too. That's probably why we conflict sometimes. People complain about me and say 'Oh, you're such a strong person, Sally', but I mean, look what I grew up with!" (Rutherford 100). What is the matriarchal society she refers to? In connection with "matriarchy," however, not much overt reference seems to emerge from the other autobiographies under review here. In fact, as in other instances of matriarchal societies, it is not unlikely that even here the phenomenon is neither always clear nor really prevalent across Australia. Patsy Cohen and Margaret Somerville, through the life stories of the five black matriarchs, try to construct the history of matriarchy in Aboriginal societies. The white colonisation brought tremendous changes and in a way it also contributed to "silence and secrecy" about traditional knowledge. Apparently, it was women like the five matriarchs who provided black women support in the period of rapid social change during the colonial period and the encouragement to "keep the culture going." Aboriginal men had lost their status and in many ways their purpose in life:

> The story of the five matriarchs is not one of loss but of physical and cultural survival. They did, in fact, pass on to their granddaughters much of the knowledge, skills and beliefs that were essential elements in their culture. These elements remain today to inform and provide a resource for Aboriginal people for the ongoing construction of their cultural reality. (Cohen and Somerville 110-11)

In fact, it is verv interesting that, on the other hand, Anne Brewster quotes Jan Pettman's warning in *Living in the Margins* against romanticising Aboriginal women as matriarchs because to do so may conceal the pressure on Aboriginal families and overestimate the ability of Aboriginal women to protect and sustain themselves and their families. Brewster reasserts Jan Pettman's argument by saying, "We need to remember that the 'black matriarchy' is a product of the poverty-induced conditions of a racially oppressed proletarian subgroup" (1995: 44). Certain examples of opinion in this issue are available, for instance, in the article "Bloodlines—not extinguishment" Kathy Malera-Bandjalan says:

> Malera people are grandmother's law. We come from the grandmother's blood line. The Malera are a matrilineal nation. That means that everything connected to Malera is connected by grandmother's law. The men, the children, the Earth, the sky, the rivers, the creeks, and the sun and moon. It goes back four generations, on the women's side. (Reed-Gilbert 64)

It should be clear, then, that we may find the discussion of this subject mired in questions such as whether we are dealing with "matriarchy" or a simpler case of "matrilineal" authority, and so on.

Let us, however, take note of a statement by the Aboriginal activist Hillary Saunders: "In the black movement there is one thing that is very hard for black women. We—and I'm saying we because I know of other black women it has happened to—are sort of shot down from both sides" (Gilbert 1977: 91). This should be read in the light of the fact that majority of the Aboriginal writers are activists. Hillary Saunders says that, all the same, it is very difficult for a black woman to be a part of the black movement. If she did have matriarchal status, it seems of no consequence in this context. In actuality, black women seem to have had the worst of the bargain. A black woman is shot down in black movements because of two factors, that is her race and her gender. Her race faces dangers and antagonism outside but her gender subjects her to difficulties from both within and outside her society. Although they have to face such difficulties and discouragement from two sides, Aboriginal women's writing really does not spell out the suffering within. There is an absolute silence regarding the exploitation within Aboriginal society. Critics like Diane Bell interpret this exploitation within as the influence of white woman's image. It has also been related to the frustrations of Aboriginal man because of discrimination in society. Both the viewpoints implicitly ignore the fact that, by and large, it was the white man who may have also influenced the colonised Aborigines most. Whatever may be the truth regarding glorification of the image of Aboriginal woman within Aboriginal societies, the stark reality of colonial and postcolonial society is that Aboriginal woman has to face ill-treatment from white society

Sally Morgan persuades her grandmother to narrate her story. With much difficulty, convinced by others that Aborigines ought to narrate their stories from their point of view, she speaks out. But still she keeps some secrets to herself, such as her having had other children, apart from Sally Morgan's mother, who had been removed from her. When asked about this, she is terribly upset. It is not uncommon for Aboriginals to attempt to maintain privacy and full control over one's thoughts, feelings, experiences and expressions.

Sally Morgan pleads with her to narrate everything; for not knowing extorts its own price: "It's not a matter of secrets, Nan. . . . You seem to be ashamed of your past, I don't know why. All my life, you've never told me anything, *never let me belong to anyone*" (Morgan 148; my italics). Ironically, Sally Morgan's grandmother secretly fears that revealing Sally Morgan's identity may lead to the family's disowning of the children. Despite Sally Morgan's assurance that she need not be ashamed of her past, she cannot but be ashamed. This kind of adverse effect on questions of Aboriginal identity often arises on account of white people's attitudes.

* * * * *

In her autobiography, Ruby Langford Ginibi says that there are three types of Koori people in Australia: the traditional tribal people, mission-bred ones like her, and urban Koori. But she considers them all one "mob." Although Ruby Langford Ginibi attempts to revive a spirit of unity, women's autobiographies offer a complex and complicated pattern of multiple identities and serious identity crises, as we have seen in our discussion so far. Some Aboriginal women writers clearly dissociate themselves from the groups with which they are identified by whites. This gives rise to a very interesting discussion about the difference between the writers' perception of their identity and society's perception of their identity. Consider Alice Nannup's case. In *When the Pelican Laughed*, she presents a description of her multiple identity; she refers to her being a North-Wester as well as an international person. Obviously, Nannup is a woman, an Aboriginal woman, an Aboriginal and a North-Wester. What is her country, North-West Australia or Australia? Does her North-Wester identity set her apart from Aborigines of other parts of Australia?

Another such instance occurs in Ella Simon's *Through My Eyes*. On the subject of white man's diseases that spread among the Aborigines, she says, "it used to hurt so much when people treated me as though I was one of these old tribal people" (Simon 4). If it hurts her when she is considered "one of these old tribal people," where does she belong? A new tribal or not a tribal at all? If it hurts her to be identified with Aboriginal people, how does she justify her

Aboriginal consciousness in her autobiography? In another context, Ella Simon herself puts the problem across succinctly:

> If it hadn't been for my grandmother I might well have been brought up as a white. But that doesn't mean to say that I was accepted by the Aborigines, either. Well, I was more than half white, so where was I, half white and half black, supposed to go? Where was I supposed to fit in? (13)

This dilemma of belonging neither here nor there seems to be one of the major problems before Aboriginal women writers. Half-white and half-black, firmly or clearly accepted by neither black nor white people, where *does* Ella Simon fit in? And where does she *want* to fit in? Her statement also reveals that she is not seen as black, would have passed for a white but for her grandmother. Obviously, her colour also matters in formulating her attitude towards Aboriginal issues because if she could "pass" for a white, she might be accepted by mainstream society. That would nullify the conflict of identity in her. But does it really happen?

Oppression and discrimination can induce a defensiveness and inferiority complex in the oppressed. This may give rise to a conscious disavowal of membership of the stigmatised group. Ella Simon often separates herself from Aborigines; Daisy and Gladys, in their turn, deny to Sally Morgan that they are indigenous women. The overt denial of indigenous identity by these indigenous women in certain contexts, however, does not disrupt their socio-cultural practices in other contexts. To quote Aileen Moreton-Robinson, "Indigenous women's subjectivity has been shaped by historically imbued representations of Indigeneity developed in anthropological and legal discourses as much as by Indigenous discourse of self-presentation" (29).

Compared to these issues and discussions, the identity crisis of Roberta Sykes as it is revealed in her three-volume autobiography *Snake Dreaming* seems to be much more intense and disturbing. Her identity is ambiguous not only to herself but also to the readers. Yet for the society around her, she remains a black and she is judged by the white society around her as a natural target of its prejudices. Her identities, therefore, seem to shift according to her changing perceptions of herself and yet society's perception of her identity refuses to change. As a black, she is always looked upon with suspicion and mistrust. Because she is black, she is gang-raped. She is almost killed only because of her "blackness." After this incident, perversely, the identity of a licentious woman is also added to her black identity. Her post-rape trauma, her staying away from men, are interpreted as inclination towards lesbianism; some women actually make advances to her. Yet she is recognised as a snake woman by some Aboriginal people who identify her with the snake people from the North. Even the fierce dogs attack her without the least provocation from her.

While her identity as a black is so clearly, variously or even perversely recognised by society, Roberta Sykes herself reels under the contradictions implicit in her confused and multiple identity. She knows nothing about her origin. She realises that she is different from her white mother and other white people around her and cannot identify herself with either white or black. As a helpless rape victim, she walks from hospital to police station to court, seeking audience or understanding. Not only does the rape result in trauma, eventually an unwanted child is also born. As an unwed mother, Roberta Sykes struggles in search of livelihood and self-esteem. She moves from one job to another, as a snake dancer in a nightclub and to various jobs in Aboriginal organisations. She becomes an Aboriginal activist. She even obtains a doctorate from Harvard University. But the fundamental question about her identity has dogged her life at least up to that point.

She knows little not only about her father and origin, but also about her religion. Whether her mother has a religion or not is also a question for her but she understands that her mother has a particular dislike for Catholics. Her mother, who is considered a sinner for having black children, calls Catholics hypocrites for throwing out coloured people from school when in fact they were supposed to save souls. Coming from a family based on "secrets and deceit" and without any security, Roberta Sykes recognises that she is different and can easily be picked up in a group:

> No matter that I wore the same uniform, did the same schoolwork, drank the same water and ate the same food, I was different and

> would always be different. In that flash of awareness, I realised that in my lifetime people would always see my colour first, no matter how good I was or how hard I worked, and that they'd attribute to me whatever feelings they had about people of colour. (1997: 51)

Roberta Sykes is a black according to white society and that gives rise to her multiple identities that were the lot of black people. She cites an incident from her life when the detectives encountered her:

> "Where's your pass—or are you a runaway? . . ."
>
> "Are you under the Act? What reserve are you from?"
>
> "I don't live on a reserve. I don't know what Act you're talking about. You'd better leave me alone because my mother's white." (1997: 218)

Thus, it is her mother's white identity that comes to her rescue not only here but also later when her rape criminals are punished by the court. It is a rare occurrence for white men to be punished for raping a black woman, points out Roberta Sykes. If it is her mother's white identity that comes to the rescue of Roberta Sykes and also subjects her to confusion and chaos, surely her identity is a matter of conflict.

As a rape victim, Roberta Sykes looks at herself as becoming evil, but wants to name her son Jesus for his mother had neither played a sexual role in his conception nor desired or craved for his conception. Is this an effort to identify with the Christian concepts of purity and innocence? This does not end there but proceeds to her dilemma about the priority of her son's identity:

> My search for my own identity, I realised, had to take a back seat to the construction of my child's identity and sense of self-worth. My father's identity remained unknown. Did it matter? Would my son also wonder who his father was? And what would I be able to do about that when the time came? (Sykes 1997: 326)

Ultimately, she decides not to go in search of her roots because many people who went in search of their roots broke their hearts on reaching the destination when they were not received by "their people." The other important reason is, she questions herself as to why she should search for a man, her father, who did not want to know her. She decides to stick to her Aboriginal identity, though she does not clearly know her roots, for her experience has been an Aboriginal experience:

> even though I can't prove I'm an Aborigine, you know I've been treated like an Aborigine all my life. I was put out of school, I've been insulted and abused, and even raped in terrible circumstances because those men thought I was an Aborigine. I have been arrested, and worked hard to bring about changes, a better life for us all. (Sykes 2000: 113)

On the one hand, she is told that being raped does not make her an Aboriginal. On the other hand she is also accused by Mum Shirl of choosing not to be Aboriginal and that she cannot prove she is not one. But she is accused by society of being incapable of proving her Aboriginal identity. This debate leads to the controversy about Roberta Sykes' Aboriginal identity. She is vehemently and perversely attacked and condemned for claiming Aboriginal identity.

While Roberta Sykes' autobiography presents the writer's dilemma and her conflict with the society about her black identity, the response to her autobiography triggered much more controversy about her identity. For instance, Pat O'Shane's article on Roberta Sykes raises many issues that become charges against Roberta Sykes: "For years you've traded on the public's belief that you are Aboriginal. As far as I know, you've never actually made the claim to an Aboriginal identity yourself, but yours is not the sin of commission, it is the sin of omission" (29).

Pat O'Shane continues by saying that even if the story of Roberta Sykes is believed to be true, her experience cannot stand for that of the stolen generation, thus raising questions in the reader about "the Aboriginal experience." Commending Sally Morgan for trying to lift the covers and peel the layers to expose half-truths and deceits, O'Shane finds fault with Roberta Sykes for not doing that. Based on the information given in the autobiography also, she attacks Roberta Sykes. She says that no old man in Aboriginal custom would stop to talk to a "lonely little girl" and talk to her the way he did according to Roberta Sykes. She also informs us that the Birringubba Jurn-Bindal clan people have objected to Roberta Sykes' account of the snake totem. She also finds fault with the writer for using the snake as part of her dance because it shows disrespect for the culture. She locates Roberta Sykes among people like Streten Bozic, Elizabeth Durack and Leon Carmen, who received money and fame with the help of their pretended Aboriginal identity.

This leads us into the larger controversy of assumed, attributed and acquired identities. Pat O'Shane is concerned not only about the genetic lineage of Roberta Sykes but also about her cultural awareness and commitment towards her acquired identity. While Pat O'Shane is attacking her and praising Sally Morgan for her efforts in search of her roots, Mudrooroo finds the mode of narration of Sally Morgan's search un-Aboriginal. Jackie Huggins joins him in her attack against Sally Morgan's *My Place* and its easy accessibility to non-indigenous readers. Such controversial identities lead, on the other hand, to views such as these expressed by Rosemary van den Berg. In her article "Intellectual Property Rights for Aboriginal People," she makes an appeal for intellectual property rights for Aboriginal people in order to save them from "identity thieves." She also unveils the non-indigenous identity of people like Colin Johnson, Elizabeth Durack, Leon Carmen who have proclaimed Aboriginal identity. She calls Mudrooroo an impostor of the worst kind who has used Aboriginal identity for his own ends (Reed-Gilbert 74-81).

It should not take much more than this background for us to realise that the level of expectation from *any* voice far outstrips that voice's abilities. No writer can be expected to be an anthropologist as well—she may easily misread or only partially understand, say, her tribe's mythological or historical or genetic past. In the same way, we really do need to appreciate the fact that each writer, as a person, is in a historical location which will reflect itself in her writing. When an Aboriginal writer is, for instance, deeply integrated or involved in her upbringing or influences within the dominant society, her writing may not "sound" tribal. Similarly, a woman reporting on male behaviour, especially in the past or in a semi-fictional account may not quite succeed in becoming "authentic." Such unsatisfactory features must, surely, be a professional hazard for anyone who ventures to speak or write in public. Therefore, we have a double responsibility in dealing with such representations or voices—first, certainly to keep in mind any such "problem"; and not allow it to smother or whatever else may be being expressed.

Going by the controversy about Roberta Sykes' crisis of Aboriginal identity, not only does her autobiography raise the issue of conflict within her and between her and white society, but also of conflict between her and Aboriginal society. Against the background of this controversy, does her autobiography become a kind of fiction? Is it an autobiography merely because the writer calls it so? Or fiction because it becomes manipulated against the background of the controversy? If other Aboriginal women's autobiographies flout the rigidities of the genre of autobiography consciously or unconsciously, does this controversy change the nature and description of Roberta Sykes' autobiography in the same way? Is such a mixture of genres a part of the writer's liberty or of the political discourse of Aboriginal people? What are the conflicting identities here, apart form the ones that Roberta Sykes introduces to the readers in her autobiography? Where does she fit in as the writer of autobiography and of fiction? Is the conflict between a "genuine black identity" and an acquired identity—are these the only conflicting identities or do some more identities emerge from this controversy?

* * * * *

With all this on the one hand, another sharper controversy about identities also exists. For instance, Sally Morgan, as it has been already discussed in the earlier chapters, confesses in an interview that what prevails in her autobiography is neither Aboriginal nor feminist consciousness but working class consciousness. But any reader of her autobiography will easily make out that in *My Place* Aboriginal consciousness manifests everywhere. The best evidence of this is the theme of the autobiography, that is the search for one's Aboriginal roots and the construction and assertion of Aboriginal identity. The difference between one's true identity and one's acquired identity or what one thinks is one's identity creates the conflicting identities. For instance, Sally Morgan's voice in her interview contradicts her own voice in her autobiography. She says,

> I never thought consciously from any particular perspective, like whether it was Aboriginal or feminist or social class. It just sort of got written how it happened, basically. It's really interesting when you go back. I guess when you look back you can see those things in it and people sort of intellectualise a lot about structures but a lot of it was accidental. (Bird and Haskell 8)

It is not only surprising but also confusing for the readers since *My Place* is a text written with Aboriginal consciousness and purpose however carefully it is read and analysed otherwise. In brief, the theme of the book itself is Sally Morgan's search for her Aboriginal roots and Aboriginal identity. She goes in search of "her place" as an Aboriginal and like many other Aboriginal women writers, Sally Morgan also articulates the reasons and her intentions behind writing her autobiography.

Probably, of all Aboriginal women's autobiographies, Sally Morgan's *My Place* is the best acclaimed and also the most attacked. Of all the critics it is Mudrooroo Narogin who attacks Sally Morgan most vehemently. He dismisses and discredits *My Place* as "battler genre," which is a white genre. He thinks that this genre shows little concern for the community. His major objection is that *My Place* is an individual story and the common concerns of Aboriginal community are given secondary importance. He says in *Writing from the Fringe: A Study of Modern Aboriginal Literature,* "Sally Morgan's book is a milepost in Aboriginal literature in that it marks a stage when it is considered O.K. to be Aboriginal as long as you are young, gifted and not very black. It is an individualised story and the concerns of the Aboriginal community are of secondary importance" (Narogin 1990: 149). Although Sally Morgan herself says that she wrote her autobiography with a working class consciousness, her Aboriginal consciousness is its constant companion. She perceives herself as a working class individual and her autobiography reveals her as an Aboriginal woman. But Mudrooroo classifies her as an Aborigine who is young, gifted and not very black. This is one more aspect of her identity, acquired or attributed, apart from her being recognised on the basis of her race and gender. He says that *My Place* is an individualised story, whereas Sally Morgan believes that she presents the story of her family and her readers also get the feeling that it is representative. Thus it is not only identity crisis within the writers' personalities but also a conflict about identity between writers and critics/readers that we must contend with.

It has to be remembered here that Mudrooroo Narogin, who attacks Sally Morgan for writing like whites, was himself eventually attacked for pretending Aboriginal identity. The controversy that arose around Roberta Sykes exists in the case of Mudrooroo as well. Although there are people like Ruby Langford Ginibi who support his Aboriginal identity, the controversy remains active.

In response to Bain Attwood's article, "Portrait of an Aboriginal as an Artist: Sally Morgan and the Construction of Aboriginality" (Attwood 302-18), Jackie Huggins says that though she agrees with Bain Attwood in a way, she does not want to take the criticism of Aboriginal literature from a white critic. She agrees with him when Attwood says that Sally Morgan's Aboriginality is forged throughout the creation of the text and when he compares *My Place* to a detective novel. What irks her, Huggins says, about *My Place* is its proposition that Aboriginality can be understood by all non-Aboriginal people. The greatest weakness of the book is that it requires least translation for the white readers, according to Jackie Huggins. Deciding that the white editorial intervention has desecrated *My Place*, Jackie Huggins expresses her concern over all the good bits, oral histories, going to the back of the book instead of the front. Jackie Huggins concurs with Attwood's opinion when he says, "It would seem that in seeking an answer to her mystery, Morgan has been influenced by the European discourse about Aboriginality which is dominated by anthropological images of Aborigines as 'other'" (Attwood 306). Jackie Huggins finds fault with Sally Morgan for allowing the publishers to change her work into "another gross product of miscegenation" in America. Thus, like Mudrooroo Narogin, Jackie Huggins seems to define an Aboriginal work, its incomprehensibility to the non-Aboriginal readers as one of its crucial qualities. But she adds that she detests any non-

Aboriginal defining Aboriginality for her and her race and that such a definition insults her intelligence, spirit and soul and negates her heritage (Huggins 1993: 459-64). She rightly points out, "Like racism, Aboriginality is always being theorised, intellectualised and trivialised by those who have never felt the passion, anger or the pain" (Huggins 1993: 463).

Sally Morgan's *My Place* led not only to intra-racial discourses but also to inter-racial discourses. One major attack against Aboriginal women's autobiographies is that the writers have adopted the coloniser's genre to attack the coloniser. In her article "Autobiographical Storytelling by Australian Aboriginal Women," Kateryna Olijnyk Longley observes, "Rules of authorship, ownership, and authority, for example, are so differently understood by Aboriginal people that the term *autobiography* is immediately problematised when it is used in an Aboriginal context" (Smith and Watson 371). Narogin had already raised this criticism and had provided his answer. Ngũgĩ has also touched upon this issue in defending the choice of the genre in African Literature. African writers like Ngũgĩ tried to free not only their country from British colonialism but also their culture from British cultural imperialism. They revolted against the assumed supremacy of the English language and started writing in African languages. And they also actively propagated use of African languages and abandonment of English. They emphasised the use of one's native tongue from basic education onwards. Thus they worked towards the liberation, not only of their country but also of their education, culture, language and literature, and every other possible aspect of national life. But African writers also wrote and published a great deal of literature using genres that are assumed to be English. For example, the novel is one of the most successful and powerful tools of African writers. Referring to this controversy concerning whether one should abandon the imperial language and literature or retain imperial genres, Ngũgĩ says,

> The social or even national basis of the origins of an important discovery or any invention is not necessarily a determinant of the use to which it can be put by its inheritors. . . . The social history of the world before the advent of victorious socialism was the continued appropriation of the results and the genius of the labour of millions

> by the idle classes. Why should not the African peasantry and working class appropriate the novel? (68)

Thus Ngûgî refutes such charges levelled against African writers by stating that genres cannot be owned and disowned by anyone. In these few sentences, he brilliantly sums up the world history of age-old exploitation of the working classes by the idle classes. By doing this, he declares the solidarity of the working classes, whichever race or country they happened to be part of.

Autobiography is one of the strategies that Aboriginal literature, especially women's writing, uses to express its protest against western imperialism. How far we can call these books autobiographies and how to classify the genres are also crucial questions that these autobiographies raise in the readers. How they protest against this western influence of language and literature as part of their overall protest against imperialism was discussed in detail in the second chapter. This use of western literary tradition and revolt against western imperialism simultaneously present the conflicting identities of the writers both as followers of western tradition and as rebels against western imperialism.

Apart from the adaptation of a genre, another charge levelled against Aboriginal women's autobiographies is that they present the darker side of life and the world. Critics complain that whereas the traditional Aboriginal literature celebrates, these autobiographies establish contradictory images. That is, traditional Aboriginal literature is the happy exclamation of Aboriginal women and contemporary autobiographies are complaints and critiques. An Aboriginal woman who celebrates is different from the one who complains. There is a great variance between these two and this leads to the conflicting images and identities of Aboriginal women as unveiled in traditional and contemporary Aboriginal literature. Roberta Sykes answers this criticism by wondering what there is to celebrate. Her words not only state the stand of Aboriginal women writers but also sum up the predicament of displaced Aborigines. This issue was discussed in detail in the second chapter.

To sum up the argument in Kateryna Olijnyk Longley's words:

By violating the rules of history and biography as they have developed in the West, the Aboriginal life stories allow us to stand outside those genres and so learn to read European as well as Aboriginal culture differently. . . . Further, the autobiographical narratives remind us of the oral tradition from which they have only recently been drawn and the centrality of song, ritual and storytelling in that tradition. But perhaps the most useful lesson provided by Aboriginal women's autobiography is that flexibility, specifically literary flexibility, is needed so that all genres can continue to be loosened to accommodate differences of personal and cultural vision at any time and in any place. (Smith and Watson 382-83)

NOTES

1. An instance of this concern is the Chipko Movement of tribals in North-Eastern India for preservation of forests. Under the leadership of Sunderlal Bahuguna, people actually hugged trees (this is what "chipko" means) threatened by fellers. In another case, the Narmada Valley Movement of tribals for preservation of their lands in the leadership of Medha Patkar and others in India: this movement basically opposes a "big dam" project on the Central Indian river Narmada. Subsequent to this protest movement, a high-powered British study has, indeed, identified "big dams" as disasters in waiting.
2. For further support, see: John Moriarty, *Saltwater Fella* (Ringwood: Viking, 2000), p. 41; Kerry Reed-Gilbert, *The Strength of Us as Women: Black Women Speak* (Charnwood: Ginninderra Press, 2000), pp. 21-22; Ross Bowden and Bill Bunbury, *Being Aboriginal: Comments, Observations and Stories from Aboriginal Australia* (Sydney: ABC Enterprises, 1990), p. 17; Evelyn Crawford, *Over My Tracks: a remarkable life* (Ringwood: Penguin Australia, 1993), pp. 26-40; Monica Clare, *Karobran: the story of an Aboriginal girl* (Chippendale: Alternative Publishing Cooperative, 1978), p. 86; Mudrooroo, *US MOB: History, culture, struggle: An introduction to Indigenous Australia* (Sydney: Angus and Robertson, 1995), pp. 193-219; Oodgeroo Noonuccal, *Stradbroke Dreamtime* (Sydney: Harper Collins, 1992), p. 4; Rita Huggins and Jackie Huggins, *Auntie Rita.* (Canberra: Aboriginal Studies Press, 1996), pp. 7-8; Alice Nannup, Lauren Marsh and Stephen Kinnane, *When the Pelican Laughed* (South Fremantle: Fremantle Arts Centre Press, 1992), p. 217.

Conclusion

It is difficult to conclude a study of a contemporary and in many ways a controversial subject like Aboriginal women's autobiographies. Particularly difficult it is to arrive at definitive views or judgements because a great number of issues emerge from a study like this and there is a danger of omitting, misinterpreting or misrepresenting some. But keeping in mind that no study can be complete and perfect, an attempt is made here to indicate at least some tentative conclusions as well as point to a few directions which a study of this kind may lead us to.

In this concluding chapter, Australian Aboriginal men's autobiographies are briefly brought in so as to help contextualise the women's work. A substantial comparison between these two sets of writing will not fit in the present study of Aboriginal women's personal narratives, which have been the focus of this book. The comparison indicated here does not mean to dismiss men's writing, or to make sweeping generalisations about it, but only to set down a few of the more significant areas of difference between attitudes and values that characterise the women's as opposed to the men's writing.

In the same spirit, and to open up the possibility of future work, at the end of the chapter, a subject that holds tremendous potential for comparison is brought in, that is, women's autobiographical writing from the Aboriginal and otherwise oppressed communities in India, generally identified by the term "Dalit."

Before that, it will be worthwhile bringing together what we have encountered in our survey of Australian Aboriginal women's autobiographical writing. First of all, all the basic issues and concerns of people in comparable situations to theirs—predictable, yet most significant concerns—are found in their work. How are women treated? What roles did they play in traditional "native" societies? How do women perceive their traditional roles? How are "native" women treated in situations of large scale colonisation? By the native men, by native communities? And most crucially, by the colonising race or community? How did the women react to their treatment? Did their situation change over time? Why? Did it improve, or become worse?

In this set of general questions that confront the women writers examined in this book are included more specific questions. What was the case of their gender? Did it become a special locus of exploitation? How did their emotional nature fare in encounters with white people? How did their 'original' womanly aspirations fare? Were they assigned new roles, and if so, what were they and how did they reiterate the colonial situation? Did they, in fact, remain on the fringes of the colonial situation or did they become the locus of a major facet of colonisation? What were the deprivations imposed on them? Physically, socially, emotionally, economically, spiritually, sexually, in terms of class and gender, as mothers and wives? Did they gain anything or lose everything as colonisation progressed? What was the tenor of their consciousness of such deprivation and oppression?

This book has also tried to raise and answer questions such as: How do the above mentioned and many other related concerns and issues reflect the standpoint of Aboriginal women in a colonised situation? How does autobiography as a genre help them? How do they mend and bend the form autobiography, to suit their purposes? How and why does "silence" play such a crucial role in Aboriginal women's lives—traditional and colonised—and literature? How do their strategies in all these contexts contribute to Aboriginal women writers' effort to protest against discrimination and exploitation in the form of autobiography? Do their lives become texts for others or messages? When an autobiography deals with the writer's effort to conceal facts which are revealed to readers, as is the case of Roberta Sykes, what is the function of such an autobiography?

What kind of a self-identity do these writers construct and what are the voices that speak in the process of its definition? What is the consciousness that motivates them and guides them? Where does their identity crisis in a colonised society lead them to? What are the conflicts that prevail in their lives between them and the society, and within themselves? What kind of an impact do controversies about their Abcriginal identity have on their identity crisis? When they write, are they trying to enrich literature, construct history, deconstruct white versions of everything that is "Aboriginal"?

These and related questions are tackled by the autobiographies examined in this book. No two works are identical; no two women report the same life, the same viewpoint, or the same answers to these and other questions. Each has a significantly individual and valid viewpoint as well as world-view. The world-view, among other things, is a particularly significant aspect of these works—for it is in this that the women definitely link their current state and status with their traditional "Ab-original" situation. It is this that brings in the whole range of questions and topics we have listed, from family to spiritual affairs, loss of freedom to loss of language. It is also this factor that allows these writers to explore avenues of reaction, to participate, in varying degrees, in the process of self-definition and protest against being externally defined.

The autobiographies studied in this process bring to light the crucial fact that no matter where a genre originates, in practice an indigenously engendered work always modifies it significantly. That is why, once again, in a considerable variety, we find the women's works ranging from fictionalised autobiography to indirectly reported autobiographical reminiscence. The content, too, varies considerably between works, from reconstruction of several generations to recollection of parts of individual lives, from attention to individual experience to family experience, from cases of awful upbringing to worse adulthood. Everywhere, yet without repetitiousness, are to be encountered the language and forms of rememoration, recovery and reconstruction discovered by these writers to fit their bewilderment, pain, suffering, deprivation, ill-treatment and exploitation. These facts do not come before us as types or statistics but are recorded in voices that speak with poignant individuality, so that even omissions silently signal suffering or protest.

The works examined reveal the independence that typifies women's writing elsewhere as well—each writer, regardless of consequences in terms of reception, sets down the degree of pain, suffering and protest or accommodation she feels. None attempts to fit any literary or social mould, therefore the works are refreshing eye-openers even when at times the "contents" appear similar or familiar. Different ages are represented in these works, different degrees of distance from the dominant mainstream society, different degrees of closeness with Aboriginal origins, different degrees of consciousness of that origin and of questions of identity that arise from having a long history that was first rudely disrupted by colonials and then equally rudely kick-started in a new game of oppressor-oppressed. From the near hatred to overt assimilationist tendencies, the women's reactions, too, vary greatly. From activism to near-fatalism, we find the attitudes speaking to us in more than one voice, the apparent voice of the surface of the text, and the many, changing, unsettled, unsettling, defined, undefined voices that emerge from between the lines of these autobiographies.

It seems clear from this study that this writing by Aboriginal women must be treated as a significant body of expression of the Aboriginal situation that will yield a great deal of understanding of "how it was" and "how it is" for Aboriginal women and Aboriginal people in Australia. Without thorough consideration of both the contents and the voices in these autobiographies, any study of the general Aboriginal situation will remain grossly incomplete. Although such is the case wherever women's voices are concerned, in any time or community or predicament, for an appreciation of what has happened during the past 200 years in an island that had been inhabited by its "natives" during the hundred thousand years that preceded the colonial experience, these works are indispensable. What these works add no other works can, the viewpoints about Aboriginal situation that they make available will not be available elsewhere. What is available in the form of autobiographies and autobiographical fiction helps reconstruct, correct, revise history successfully, to add those aspects of that history which are missing from or distorted in "the Australian history."

Even as the Aboriginal women's autobiographies studied here discuss history, identity, conflict and consciousness in a protesting voice, there is a sense in which all of them also attempt a reconciliation with the facts that they may have to co-exist with whites, and that neither a policy of "back to the roots" nor an attempt at total independence as an Aboriginal Australia is likely to work. But their uncompromising demand is for equality and justice. It is therefore not surprising that Aboriginal women's autobiographies are sometimes criticised for being accommodative or that there is a feeling that they either accept or seek to come to grips with white dominance. It is also said that Aboriginal affairs are entering a stage of post-activism in that the emphasis is on "sharing and understanding" rather than on justice. Sally Morgan's *My Place*, in particular, has been attacked for being a personal history only, and not a part of a general Aboriginal movement. But all Aboriginal women writers—except perhaps Shirley Smith, who says that she does not understand the relationship between Aborigines and politics even though she is actually associated with politics—have declared that to be born an Aborigine is political and that the personal is also political. Neither *My Place* nor any other Aboriginal woman's autobiography deals merely with the past nor is any of them a "death book," to use Mudrooroo Narogin's term. For, all these autobiographies reveal hatred of injustices committed against Australian Aborigines, agony for the deplorable colonial past, as well as hope for the future. They express anguish for the deaths and look forward to births. Thus these autobiographies are books of commitment to life and future.

There is certainly a voice in these autobiographies that speaks of reconciliation and co-existence. For instance, while Sally Morgan clearly voices the urge for reconciliation in her *My Place*, Alice Nannup, in her autobiography *When the Pelican Laughed*, bemoans the fact that in Australia equality was seen only during wartime years: "because they were in uniform, those boys were allowed to go and drink in a bar with the white soldiers. They all reckoned wartime was the only time they ever felt they were equal" (Nannup 174). This statement, apart from pointing out the discrimination, clearly and strongly implies a wish for equality in peacetime as well. There may be sarcasm in the statement about the government's policy of implementing equality, but it definitely insists on a permanent equal status for Aborigines. Aborigines have fought in the war on behalf of the white government yet Alice Nannup does not even question the decision that made Aborigines participate in the war, only the temporary status of the "equality."

Ida West's version of Aboriginal participation in the war presents another dimension of the relations between Aborigines and the white government. In *Pride against Prejudice*, she speaks proudly about Aboriginal participation in the war and her brother's shaking hands with the Prime Minister. Such instances are examples of the writer's wish for Aboriginal people to be equal citizens in Australia, and show an attachment to the concept of the Australian nation. She throws light on the aim the Aboriginal movement and its literature may pursue: "Yes, it's going to be a long time before we all can be on even terms with the Europeans, not that we want to be any better but just so we can speak and try to do our work and have our own land" (West 47). There is, however, much more to this. For, at the same time, this attitude can be traced to the implicit Aboriginal concept of man belonging to the land and not the land belonging to man. The works of the writers examined in this book assert that they are fighting against racial discrimination and not white imperialism.

In *Stradbroke Dreamtime*, Oodgeroo Noonuccal laments:

> The island is different now. Civilisation and man's greed have chased away our shy nautilus shells. Motorcars belch fumes over the land, and the noise of industry drowns out all other sounds of life. Men's machines have cut and maimed and destroyed what used to be.
>
> Stradbroke is dying. The birds and animals are going. The trees and flowers are being pushed aside and left to die. Tourists come to soak up the sunshine and bathe in the blue Pacific, scattering as they go their discarded cans and cigarette packs and bottles and even the hulks of cars.
>
> Greedy, thoughtless, stupid, ignorant man continues the assault on nature. But he too will suffer. His ruthless bulldozers are digging his own grave. (1972: 4)

In this elaborate and heart-rending description, nowhere do we find an overt reference to racial conflict and imperialism but only to the untoward impact of European civilisation. It is implied that this so-called civilisation was introduced and established by whites. Nor is there any reference to the original white invasion of Aboriginal land. Thus it once again proves that her voice is raised not against the whites as a race and as invaders, but only against the attitude and world-view of the whites. Her statement in her interview with Gerry Turcotte, "Recording the Cries of the People," in which she says that decent people have been her audience, supports this. She elaborates this by her reference to "whites as well as blacks. The humanitarians—who wanted to know more about the Aboriginals—welcomed it [her writings] with open arms" (Rutherford 19). The question *Is That You Ruthie?* reasserts the purpose and inspiration of Aboriginal writing and the repeated and reiterated Aboriginal experience. Ruth echoes here the same spirit of Aboriginal writing:

> This book, however, was, never intended to place blame, but to record our experiences and to remember the past for the sake of all who lived through it. I cry when I remember my sisters, we would be a forgotten generation if I didn't write about what we experienced. I write for them so that their lives and the treatment they received will always be remembered. (Hegarty 43)

When asked about the Aboriginal struggle against the whites, citing the example of India's freedom struggle, Roberta Sykes says, "I think Aboriginal people are realistic. And there is no point in wanting to put the sun in your pocket. And so you have to have achievable goals. And I don't think that the white people are going to go. Largely because they don't have anywhere to go to. You can't squash 18 million people back into Europe" (Personal Interview, 9 January 1998).

On the other hand, there is a conscious effort from within the movement to convince the readership that not all whites are prejudiced and discriminating. Whether it is the writer's own voice or the interference of the editor, this kind of an establishment of the concept of "good whites" may also be perceived in some of the Aboriginal women's autobiographies. Monica Clare's autobiographical novel *Karobran,* edited and "improved" by Jack Horner, is the best example of this. The narration is quite interesting in the sense that it presents white atrocities and immediately tries to argue that not all whites discriminate against the Aborigines. This does not happen only once but repeatedly, wherever there is scope. This proves the writer's or improver's desperate attempt to prove that she is not arguing against the whole white community but only against atrocious and discriminating whites and specifically government policies. In *Karobran*, the descriptions of dry, muddy and dirty land where the reserves for Aborigines are built, starvation, suffering, illiteracy and poverty that prevail among the Aborigines are countered by statements like this: "sometimes she would feel like shouting at them, when they would tell her how much they had come to hating white people for ever coming to this country. She knew that she could tell them about people like Aunt, Uncle and Bill" (Clare 87-88). Whether the writer attempted to suppress this protest or the editor does so may remain beyond the reach of the reader, for the writer is no longer alive and the work has been interfered with. When Isabelle, towards the end of the novel, declares that Aborigines should make the whites understand that Aborigines are not children and that they are capable of looking after themselves, we can ironically hear an acceptance of the need to be heard and understood by the whites. It only acknowledges that they are convinced that they are taken care of by whites as children are cared for by parents or elders. It may have cropped up due to the writer's experience and opinion and her identity as a lighter complexioned Aboriginal girl; yet at the same time there is every chance of the editor's opinions and intentions having crept in.

There is a clear urge for reconciliation and co-existence in Monica Clare's words when she says, "Isabelle needed no reassurance from her Mum's people like Aunt, Uncle and Bill, who she knew would teach their young children to understand that black was not a dirty word, and that together with white it would mean strength for equality and human rights" (94). It is not a condemnation of whites' attitude towards the word black and the existence of blacks. It is, however, an attempt at convincing herself of the greatness of the word black and it is an attempt at amalgamation of the two colours. The voice of the narrator changes as we enter the second part of the book. In the first, we come across a clear condemnation of the discriminatory policy of the whites and the white government and specifically white attitudes towards blacks. But gradually this condemnation limits itself to one section or type of whites who inflict inhuman treatment on the blacks. In the first half too we find white characters who are generous and understanding, and the characters who haunt us are those who, like Tom, harass the innocent children due to their prejudice against the blacks. There is only an indirect argument or evidence of the small section of whites who take care of Aborigines, like Uncle, Aunt, Tom's wife and others. Also, in the second part, apart from this, there is a direct argument in favour of the whites. The reasons and factors behind this are debatable and throw a provocative riddle before the reader. On the one hand, many of the women writers are also active protestors against both colonial invasion of native life as well as discrimination. On the other there are writers like Monica Clare who seem to suggest that the wrong is neither very deep nor particularly humiliating. This situation of loud and angry protest riding alongside assimilationist tendencies clearly parallels that in the history of many other colonised countries' reaction to domination by outsiders.

Anita Heiss articulates the intentions behind Aboriginal women's writing and her words may provide us with a clue to some of the mysteries mentioned above in Aboriginal women's writing:

> I have gained an insight into the reasons why black women have chosen to take up the pen instead of the sword in order to win our war.
>
> Our war is sometimes against the ignorant non-Indigenous population. Sometimes it's a war against our own emotions and thoughts. At other times it's a war against the man who's been beating them for too long. For some, at times like me, it's a war against the wahgin (white woman) at school who thought she was better than anyone else. (Reed-Gilbert 37)

Thus, it is a war not so much against colonisation as against discrimination. While it has not been possible in the present study to compare Australian Aboriginal women writers' role in such protest with women writers with similar backgrounds like African American, Native American, Native Canadian, Maori and Indian Dalit, that would be a study worth undertaking. Similarly, to understand the specific reasons why Aboriginal women writers in Australia leaned towards milder forms of protest than militancy, again in comparison with the other above-mentioned situations, would also be worth study.

* * * * *

Although it is not only gender consciousness that dominates Aboriginal women's autobiographies, these autobiographies can uniquely be distinguished from men's autobiographies, in their concerns and perceptions from women's point of view. Now, to change direction, Aboriginal women's autobiographies and the issues that they raise provoke thoughts in readers about Aboriginal men's autobiographies as well. At some stage it would become inevitable to look at men's autobiographies alongside the women's, since they might provide material for a more complete Aboriginal perspective of their own predicament between the two worlds.

The basic questions that emerge when we look at Aboriginal writing divided as men's writing and women's writing are: What is the effect of the gender identity of the Aboriginal writers according to themselves and according to society? How do the men writers identify themselves with Aboriginal women as a class? Who do they identify themselves with, Aboriginal women or white men? What is the purpose and function of Aboriginal men in writing their autobiographies? Does their memory work selectively in their autobiographies? Which phases of their lives are "selected out" and which become the central point of their autobiographies and why? Where do they locate themselves as Aborigines, as men and as Aboriginal men?

When we consider these questions and others that come up when we compare Aboriginal men's and women's writing, more differences can be perceived than similarities. For instance, in his autobiography *A Bastard like Me,* Charles Perkins describes how Aboriginal children were prevented from entering Alice Springs except on Saturday nights. He focuses here on the geographical, social and racial boundaries that were created for Aboriginal people. He introduces himself as a stolen child, dormitory boy, "half-caste," "scum," and "unwanted" in white society. He is a "half-caste," and therefore belongs to nobody and nowhere. He identifies himself with other "half-castes" like him who feel that something is wrong with them, that something is missing in them. They are all dissatisfied with most things in life. Having been identified by white society as a bastard, the worst of both the worlds, Perkins longs to be recognised as a human being.

Such are the common issues that both Aboriginal men's and women's writing raise and throw light on and which are of great concern to them. But, for the rest, men writers take a different view of the Aboriginal situation. While the women writers, by and large, keep silent about the internal problems of Aboriginal and mixed blood societies, men writers sharply criticise the attitude of the mixed blood people towards Aboriginal people, apart from discussing their trauma of belonging to neither Aboriginal societies nor to white society. It is very interesting that Charles Perkins distinguishes his Arunta tribe from other Aboriginal tribes on the ground that his tribe is more flexible in its attitude towards whites and it can easily admit whites into its society without any grief or vacillation. But he does not raise the question whether the whites are ready or willing to be admitted into Aboriginal societies or whether the whites are ready to accept the Arunta tribe into their society.

Not only does Perkins assert the flexibility of his tribe, he also attacks the attitude of the mixed blood people towards Aboriginal societies. Perkins says, "Unfortunately some part-Aborigines resent and even hate the fact of their existence. I know of many in Alice Springs alone who are ashamed of their ancestry and condemn at every opportunity tribal relatives or people. I feel sorry for them. They are lost people" (11). He also reveals that many part-Aborigines are very vocal in condemning tribal or other Aborigines. They relish the thought that between them and the gutter there is somebody, the Aboriginal people. On the other hand, he says that most "half-castes" hate Aboriginal people because that is what the government wants. He also recollects his childhood as a dormitory boy during which the children were not allowed to meet Aboriginal people and were cut off from tribal life. In that case, is he different from mixed blood people who move away from tribal societies? Is it not a part of the conditioning, as he himself says, of Aboriginal people to admire whites and hate their own people? Although women writers also hint that there are differences among Aboriginal people, they do not really devote much space to these attitudinal problems of "half-caste" people towards Aboriginals and tribals, except referring to the struggle of the mixed blood people to fit into the white society and their anxiety about not being admitted into Aboriginal society.

Against this background, it is worth noticing how Charles Perkins looks at Aboriginal women: "The pioneer men decided to get rid of all the dark women they were having relationships with, women who had helped them build their cattle stations up to what they were" (10). Apart from revealing Perkins' historical consciousness, the above statement reveals his awareness of the predicament of Aboriginal women. He tries to define an Aboriginal motherhood on the basis of Aboriginal mothers' suffering at the deaths of their children by saying that they suffer great emotional strain and physical injury, thus creating a separate category of Aboriginal motherhood. But, when he refers to his own affairs, he states that Australian girls bore him to tears because they are crude and common, lacking class and warmth. Yet in no other way does he refer to his association with Aboriginal girls. When he says that white girlfriends were ashamed of Aboriginal boys and were scared to meet them in open, he does not even refer to his response to Aboriginal girls or their response to him. Does he deliberately ignore his association with or his reactions to Aboriginal girls? Why does he create boundaries between himself and Aboriginal girls? Does the fact that he subsequently married a white woman influence this part of his life? Does it give rise to selective memory?

In some ways, Perkins speaks with the same militant spirit that pervades Aboriginal women's writing when he says that the more the whites criticise the Aboriginal people the more determined he is to learn to fight them and answer their irrational criticism. But his general approval and support of England also raises several questions about the factors that contribute to his opinions. Does he forget that Australian whites were descendants of migrants from England? Does he ignore the attitude of the British towards blacks in England? Again, is it his location in white society that influences his opinions about the British?

John Moriarty is another Aboriginal writer who expresses his admiration for England in his autobiography *Saltwater Fella*: "If you were a likeable person, they didn't discriminate on colour—at least the people I met didn't" (Moriarty 137). What does likeable mean? Likeable to whom? Does likeable mean successful? Does it mean unresentful and docile? Who are these "people" he refers to? Surely, many other factors besides being "likeable" are involved in interracial encounters. So, can the attitude he reports be taken as the general British attitude towards coloured people?

Of mixed blood, a stolen and dormitory boy like Charles Perkins, John Moriarty also presents both his childhood and adulthood during which he faces discrimination and adverse conditioning at every step. As a child he has been told, "You must forget your language, your culture and things like that. Stop acting like an uncivilised Aborigine" (Moriarty 18). Like any other institutionalised Aboriginal child, John Moriarty was also conditioned to forget his language, culture and people. This made him express his concern, as an insider, for the predicament of Aboriginal people and anger towards the attitude of the government:

> Governments, both State and Federal, didn't acknowledge our most basic rights—they still had a policy of assimilation. Before that, their policy had been to "smooth the dying pillow." They thought we were all going to die out, and that the aim, therefore, was to make our extinction as painless as possible. At various times we were classified as full-bloods, half-castes, quarter-castes, octoroons—all measures of blood and various shades of colour which determined how an individual was treated. Full-blood? Left to die. Half-caste like me? Taken. Quarter-caste or octoroon? Taken sooner. (Moriarty 176)

Like Charles Perkins, Moriarty also reveals that, being a "half-caste," he was refused by the girls. Only his identity as a successful soccer player brought him what he had lost as a half-caste. Like a typical Aboriginal person, he emphasises the importance of home, security, sense of belonging and reiterates that their home is their Aboriginal culture.

It is very interesting and important that he creates his identity. He is a "half-caste" stolen boy who is in search of his parents and roots. He locates his mother, who is an Aboriginal, and also his father's people in Ireland. In a way it is a typical Aboriginal writer's search for roots. But recollection is different from other Aboriginal writing, especially women's writing, because the writer here also goes in search of his white roots. Interestingly, he tries to connect Aboriginal people with the Irish in their attitudes, saying that the Irish, like the Aboriginal people, accept relatives irrespective of their colour.

Although his own sense of identity is very clear to him, the question as to who he identifies with remains unanswered. He fails to get along with an Aboriginal girl and comes to the conclusion that Aboriginality cannot be the only factor that binds two people, and so he marries a white woman and lives happily ever after. Here it seems as though he is speaking as a man rather than as an Aboriginal man. It seems as if he is trying to create another category within that of Aboriginals with reference to his contemporaries who failed to identify with their Aboriginality as he did and were terrible failures in life: "Maybe it is a little simplistic, but part of me wonders whether they got into difficulties because they couldn't find the inner serenity that would enable them to take pride in their Aboriginal heritage." (Moriarty 272). Is this an un/conscious attempt to blame Aboriginal people instead of finding the loopholes and injustice in the system? Is he trying to elevate himself above common Aboriginal people?

Already Moriarty is different from other Aboriginal people in the sense that he is a well-known soccer player, a businessman and a successful individual. He is not every Aboriginal person but a rare and outstanding example. Apart from material achievements, is he in his argument trying to claim spiritual achievements? He reveals that successful people are always acceptable and there are many film stars, sport stars and businessmen who are black and yet well accepted into white society. But the question is, is it fair to determine acceptability on the basis of such extraordinary examples of success? Is Moriarty happy because he and a very few people like him are successful and so are accepted in society? Does he feel or express concern for those who are not successful for various reasons and hence are not accepted in or by white society? Once again, any genuine enlightenment regarding such attitude seems to be conspicuous by its absence in the writing of Aboriginal women.

In the same manner, Charles Perkins also stands out from fellow Aboriginal people in general. He is a reputed soccer player, an activist, and successful in life and powerful in politics. Can he, then, represent every Aboriginal man's experience and expression? Perkins himself pinpoints his extraordinary status: "First Aborigine out of university. First Aborigine in a professional soccer team. First Aborigine to work overseas in a coalmine. First Aborigine to lead the Freedom Rides and now . . . first on the kidney machine!" (151). This is not, even if in the end it becomes a little sarcastic, a voice that speaks on behalf of the experience of the community. This is not the voice that identifies with every black man/woman. In this aspect of Aboriginal writing, too, the women seem far more concerned about and involved with the life and situation of the Aboriginals as a community, as a race. Their gender concerns do not, obviously, overshadow their community concerns, as the men's seem to do. One may even venture the possibility that it is gender that allows the women to extend their interest beyond individuality, given their traditional role and responsibilities. At any rate, all the women's autobiographies examined in the present book evince concern for the overall situation of Aboriginal people in Australia.

Women writers differ from men writers also in their discussion of sex and sexuality. While women writers elaborate only sparingly on their affairs and sexual abuses, men writers treat at length and in detail their affairs and advances to girls, their disappointments and frustrations in love life. As it has been discussed in earlier chapters, women writers do not cross these boundaries as far as sex and sexuality are concerned. Jackie Huggins declares, "Until there is a real understanding of racism in this country and genuine moves made towards racial equality, many Aboriginal women will not be prepared to talk publicly, to audiences of 'others', about the oppression they suffer through sexism" (35). Although Roberta Sykes is more overt while discussing these issues compared to other women writers, in her case it may be an attempt to liberate and detach herself from the trauma of rape. While men writers express anxiety regarding being accepted in white society, women writers protest against their not being acceptable in white society despite being victims of sexual abuse and exploitation by white males. They express far greater anxiety about not being accepted by or being alienated from mainstream society—in fact, they seem genuinely concerned about belonging to Aboriginal society. They attack the other's discriminatory attitude, of all white society.

If Aboriginal consciousness is expressed in women writers' search for their roots, is it a consciousness tinged with dominant white attitudes that is expressed in men writers' search for roots? What is the purpose of men writers in writing their autobiographies? It certainly does not seem to be to record collective experiences the way women like Ruth Hegarty do in their autobiographies. The men's narratives, by and large with exceptions like Mudrooroo Narogin's autobiographical fiction, seem to bring us individual experiences of successful people who have gained acceptability. They seem to function more as inspiration for Aboriginal people towards assimilation and reconciliation. Although Mudrooroo Narogin attacks women's writing for being favourable to assimilation and reconciliation, it is really the men writers who seem to deserve that criticism far more.

It is therefore not surprising that John McLaren's autobiographical novel *The Sweet Water—Stolen Land*, unlike Clare's *Karobran*, presents history with the coloniser in the centre. The white man, not the Aboriginal, seems to be the real protagonist. Although the historical consciousness of the writer is commendable and his reconstruction of history deserves appreciation, it is a history that revolves round the white protagonist. The Aboriginal story remains only a sub-text in this autobiographical novel. Such is definitely not the case with Aboriginal women's autobiographical fiction.

* * * * *

It will be interesting to locate Aboriginal women's autobiographies in the general picture of the marginalised literatures. It may not be possible to comment on or analyse the situation all over the world, for marginalisation may take place on the basis of several factors in any society and in any era. At times it may have been brief; at times it may have lasted long enough to appear permanent. It may be marginalisation of individuals or it may be marginalisation of entire communities. Individuals do not belong to one single category nor do they remain in the same category forever except in some given situations in which they are, for long periods of time, discriminatorily classified by others. As we have seen in the previous chapters, Aboriginal women writers come from different backgrounds, are interested in different issues, write in different tones and have achieved different purposes. The difference may be great but Aboriginality is the uniform factor that facilitates a study of all these writers under one category.

Throughout human history, imperialism has subjected cultures and peoples to subservience that has resulted in the elimination, enslavement or degradation of indigenous peoples and cultures. These peoples and cultures, although virtually eliminated or subdued forcibly and violently, may succeed in raising a voice of protest, however faint, in spite of paradoxical efforts towards appropriation and alienation at different levels. In modern history, Native Americans, the Maoris of New Zealand, Native Canadians and many other peoples have fought the battle and are still fighting it. This battle against colonialism may, indeed, seem to have receded into the background today, but the battle against discrimination and their lament over the loss of their "original identity" still continue and provide the thrust to their movements and their literatures.

If two hundred years of colonisation, discrimination and exploitation have given rise to the present Aboriginal situation discussed in this book, what happens when some sections of society are subjugated, isolated, eliminated or oppressed, by non-European, non-white, non-technological, and pre-modern oppressors for thousands of years? This is exactly the scenario that the Indian Dalit and Tribal situation and their literatures represent. There may not appear to be any direct basis of comparison between the "Dalit" situation and Dalit literature in India and the Aboriginal situation and Aboriginal literature in Australia. Some of the issues are different, the predicaments are different and the movements are different. But colonial phenomenon presents common fact. Consequently, the voice of the suffering, discriminated and exploited people is, essentially, one and the same all over the world. It is a voice that bursts out from the crushing silence of decades, centuries or even millennia. It is a voice that heart-rendingly expresses the agony and also fiercely and indignantly expresses the protest. Indian Dalit literature and Aboriginal literature provide such a relevant context for an Indian student of Australian literature and politics of oppression.

Extending the scope from Australia to India will open up many avenues for discussion and comparison. India has gone through the stage of colonialism for several millennia. And the last two centuries of the rule of the British, will be crucial in comparison of the history of Indian and Australian Aborigines. For this is the phase during which the modern concept of the Indian nation came into existence and culminated in the freedom struggle. Like other fourth world countries, India has also suffered a crisis of loss of culture, language, lifestyle and identity. The process of at least partial absorption and assimilation, which one proclaims took place during earlier periods of colonisation, did not work with the British rule. The British always remained the "other" for Indians. Literature, life and the movements have all echoed the demand for independence from both British as well as indigenous oppression.

It may not be true that independent India is completely free from oppression. There are fourth world societies in India in the form of the castes and displaced and dispossessed Aboriginal communities. Even today, serious displacement is taking place of Aboriginal people from locations of major river dams, for instance. The caste system of India had ostracised certain sections of society as untouchables. These people are marginalised and alienated by the mainstream majority society. In order to glorify certain sections and put them on a higher pedestal, the dominant strata of society have portrayed and treated the outcastes as subhuman. In the political game of control of wealth and power, caste has been used as a weapon that has been actively and seriously bolstered by religion. Some sections like the Aboriginal people of India, on the other hand, were driven into the forests and mountains. Their situation differs significantly, therefore, from that of outcastes.

Tribal gods and goddesses have been absorbed by mainstream society. Several cultural and other practices have been assimilated.

Medicinal systems have been learnt from them. Tribal peoples and cultures throughout the length and breadth of India have contributed immeasurably to the mainstream culture and society over long stretches of time. In spite of all this, the lower caste people have always inhabited the fringes of mainstream society, always at hand to be exploited. In contrast, the tribals have always remained genuine outcastes, that is to say, they have been forced right outside the pernicious caste system also. Some have lived in reasonable isolation but total neglect; some have kept contact with mainstream society by occasionally selling forest products; some have taken up special professions (e.g., the Ramoshis of Maharashtra worked as night watchmen in villages); some have suffered directly at the hands of mainstream society, for instance by being branded as criminals. Hundreds of tribes in India have been living in forests and co-existing with beasts, experiencing poverty, suffering and diseases from times immemorial—their ways corroded, their lands encroached upon, their women raped, and in general their existence being squeezed from all sides. From this has emanated their literature, which is nothing but a record of their life and their anguished protest. Most of it being oral, it has tended to vanish with the passing of time. Whatever remains is, by and large, inaccessible because of language barriers and the thrust of the mainstream languages on the tribals.

Like other fourth world literatures, the mainly oral literature of the marginalised sections of Indian society has begun to gain momentum in the recent decades, building their movement on the pillars of protest and resistance. The term "Dalit," which means people who have been ground down, came into existence as part of this struggle for identity and restitution. Like the terms "native," "indigenous" and "Aboriginal," the term Dalit has also become debatable with some disagreements regarding inclusions and exclusions. For instance, only untouchables are Dalit according to one view; tribals, backward castes and minorities including those converted to other religions are Dalit according to another. In this process, in fact, India's Aboriginal people have been further marginalised. Despite all these sub-categories and controversies, however, still the Dalit movement and Dalit literature have grown considerably in the past three decades in the path of revolt. Whether literature is the weapon of the movement or not, the common degraded treatment and condition are inseparable, interdependent and contributory in the literature of both the caste Dalits and Aboriginal Dalits in India.

It is difficult for an outsider to deal with Dalit literature because of lack of exposure and shared experience and also because this literature is mostly written or composed not even in India's regional languages, but in the far less known Aboriginal language. This obstacle redoubles the difficulty. In spite of all these hurdles, Dalit literature has been able to capture the attention of the readers and critics and contributed to a major change in viewpoints in society and literature mainly because of a strenuous and useful translation effort.

Reference to these historical, social and political issues is inevitable when we regard these literatures, since they are the products of that background. Without an introduction to the background it would be difficult to understand and interpret these literatures, although the heartburn and outburst of suffering may be felt without even an awareness of the specific content. In comparison to caste-Dalit literature, however, Aboriginal literature has not been well documented. Consequently, contemporary Tribal literature has not yet gained momentum comparable to that of the literatures of other sections. As the Aborigines still live, by and large, in isolation from the main areas of habitation, culture and language of mainstream society, illiteracy and lack of awareness of their condition and the world outside contribute to this slowness in the movement of Tribal written literature.

Like Australian Aborigines, Indian tribals too have lost their lands, languages, cultures, liberty and identity. They do not find a proper place in "Indian" history. Although they have revolted a number of times against local kings and also the British rule, the tribals are "invisible" in history and in literature. Some of the issues that Australian Aboriginal women writers raise and for which they express concern, hold the mirror up to the tribal situation in India. For instance, the concern of the writers for the gradually disappearing Aboriginal culture and traits finds a parallel in partial tribal assimilation into the mainstream society as in general isolation from it; elimination of their culture in the name of assimilation and the disappearance of their tribal traits are other factors that are common. Ignoring their attachment to land, they are evacuated in the name of excavations, explorations and development, thus leading to displacement and dislocation. The concern that Monica Clare expresses for the displacement of Aboriginals in the name of productive projects reminds one of movements with active tribal participation in India such as the "Chipko" movement for protection of Aboriginal forests, and the "Save Narmada" agitation against displacement of tribals to make way for a major dam in Central India. The above examples provide hints as to where these two situations meet and where the need is for them to be juxtaposed in any comparative study.

Like the Australian Aboriginal people, whenever Indian tribals have been the subject of literature, they have been portrayed as subhuman or they have been glorified as noble savages. They have always been stereotypes in the minds of Indians, whose characteristics were mainly negative, human sacrifice and cannibalism being prominent among them. Their image vacillates between the noble savage and the savage strictly according to convenience or ignorance of reality. Writers like Mahasweta Devi in Bengal and V. Madgulkar in Maharashtra have helped in transforming this image into that of a human being, although an exploited human being. Still no matter how much others have written about the tribals, it is still a major drawback that no comparably powerful and assertive voice has emerged yet from the tribals themselves. There have been scanty efforts to record and publish oral literatures of the tribals.

Contemporary Dalit literature has become a force, which has shaken the foundations of caste-ridden society and literature. It has definitely contributed to a change in the attitude of society, and affected some degree of change in attitudes in literature, although it may not as yet amount to a radical reversal of the previous situation. The traditional Tribal and Dalit literatures pose problems because, like much Australian Aboriginal culture and literature, they were basically oral. Hence it was difficult to preserve them, just as it was difficult to understand them because of the language barrier. This language barrier is also still significantly imprisoning contemporary

Dalit literature. Since the literacy rate is low among Dalit people, it is not easy for them to write in mainstream regional languages. It is all the more difficult for them to publish also because most of this literature is radical in substance and rarely entertains attitudes of reconciliation. Unfamiliarity with English forces the Dalit writers to remain invisible to a large number of readers outside the regions they inhabit. There are scanty translations of Dalit literature from one Indian language into another and from Indian languages into English.

Since literary writing itself, thus, remains somewhat rare for Dalit people, writing in English becomes all the more difficult. Some regional literatures in India have accommodated Dalit literature to some extent. Within Dalit literature, again, some genres like poetry have a higher standing and are extensively written and genres like autobiography and theatre are particularly unexploited by Aboriginal literature in India. Although there is a strong and long tradition of story telling and women have always been the carriers of it, men writers dominate in number and popularity in Indian Aboriginal literatures. Not many Dalit women writers have published in regional languages and almost none in English. Hence, Dalit woman's experience in all its dimensions still needs to be expressed. For the time being, comparison may have to limit itself to caste-Dalit writing.

It is true that Dalit literature has been chiefly autobiographical. Yet Aboriginal literature has as yet only thrown up a few autobiographies. Marathi literature has dominated in writing autobiographies, including autobiographies by women. But the only autobiography by a Dalit woman translated from Marathi into English is an excerpt from the autobiography of Kumud Pawde (Dangle 1992). It is about her successful attempts to learn Sanskrit. As a Dalit and as a woman, she is twice prohibited from Sanskrit by tradition. But, she protests against this prohibition and takes a postgraduate degree in Sanskrit. It is not only her protest against this prohibition that is presented in her book but also the overt and covert discrimination and discouragement that she receives from people in her struggle to learn the classical language. In a way, however, she herself conforms the notion that Sanskrit is the supreme and sacred language that contains the treasure of knowledge even as she protests against the age-old alienation and deprivation. Thus doubly discriminated, Kumud Pawde uses a double-edged weapon against the discriminatory attitude of society. She reveals that it is not until she suffixed her upper caste husband's family name to her name that she obtained employment as a Sanskrit teacher, thus unravelling her ultimate compromise with society as a Dalit woman. Kumud Pawde chooses resistance as well as reconciliation as the theme of her autobiography.

Another Dalit woman's autobiography that has been translated into English is Bama's *Karukku* (2000) from Tamil. This autobiography brings out a different aspect of a Dalit woman's life. Like Kumud Pawde, Bama also goes in search of education, thinking that it will save her from discrimination and exploitation. When she discovers, to her utter astonishment, that such is not the case, she tries to join a nunnery, which supposedly should not be a place for differences and discrimination. Even this remains a dream for Bama because nunneries too are divided on the basis of caste that the nuns come from before their embracing Christianity. Bama remains a Dalit Christian and hence deprived of access to some of the services of the church. Disillusioned, Bama leaves the church. This is the story of a Dalit woman who tries to change her destiny by toiling hard to confront challenges. She is a Dalit woman who is not considered either as intelligent or as reliable. Her life is also the struggle of a Dalit woman who has embraced another religion in the vain hope of betterment. Bama tries to overcome the hurdle of caste discrimination by achieving "equality" with the privileged sections. But one's status in India is still dependent on the basis of one's birth and not on the basis of capabilities and achievements. Bama faces disappointment and failures at every step but refuses to give up hope and determination. Her life is an incessant struggle with the double bind of caste and gender.

Since Dalit literature is mostly written in regional languages, it will make sense here to bring in at least two contemporary Dalit women writers from Telugu, the language with which I am familiar. For instance, Challapalli Swaroopa Rani and Vinodini have raised their voice against the predicament of Dalit woman in a caste-ridden society. Although they have not written autobiographies, their poetry reaches readers as the expression of their selves. While Challapalli Swaroopa Rani presents her Dalit experience, Vinodini raises questions about her Dalit Christian identity.

Some of the issues that Dalit women's writing raises in general are those that interrogate the writer's identity. As is the case of Australian Aboriginal women writers, refusal to fit into the identity dictated by society is the primary concern of Dalit women. The black colour also represents Dalit people, their identity and their situation. Not only do they interrogate such enforced masks of identity but they also interrogate nation as negated people. Religion, which is a burden for them, becomes the greatest enemy of these Dalit women writers. Various individuals and sections depending on their locations, to be specific, have narrated "Nation" in various ways depending on their contexts. The Dalit movement and literature aim to deconstruct the very set notion of society from the viewpoint of the segregated and exploited sections and to reconstruct various aspects of Indian life from a Dalit perspective, from a marginalised people's perspective, raising a voice that has been silenced for ages. The nation that is brought into discussion is not the nation that has so far been glorified and idealised in literature and society. This is a nation, which has shamelessly disowned/alienated/ segregated /ill-treated some sections of its society, and this situation resembles both the notion of Australia as a white nation and Aboriginal women writers' protest against it.

Dalit women writers, like Australian Aboriginal women writers, feel that they cannot fit in this society, that they have no place in this society. According to them it is a country where birth decides Dalit identities and they are labelled the minute they are born. What kind of a label is it? Challapalli Swaroopa Rani says in "The Forbidden History":

> Even as I was taking shape
> in Mother's womb
> I was labelled as untouchable
> and the stamp of low-caste
> preceded my birth.
> The day I was born

> I bore the imprint of an unchaste woman
> thrown into the drainage of traditions
> and dust bin of customs.
> I became the forbidden one. (91)

This "label" reminds one of Ida West's words that every Aboriginal is born with a "handle" to one's name and Roberta Sykes' statement that whatever her capabilities, she is basically a black, and therefore different, according to whites. Challaplli Swaroopa Rani identifies herself as a Dalit woman who belongs to the country that has subjected her to the double-edged weapon of discrimination and exploitation on the basis of caste and gender and yet significantly questions the notion of such a country.

This insecurity, indignation and protest mould the writings of Vinodini as well. Her poetry bristles with the minority Christian consciousness in a majority Hindu country. Her Christian identity helps only to throw her into the world of new risks and dilemmas, apprehensions and prejudices. In her poem "All Indians are My Brothers and Sisters" (Translation unpublished) she comes across quite contrary to what her title suggests. She declares that all Indians are not her brothers and sisters. She is never treated as one of these brothers and sisters even as a Christian. She does not ignore the fact that, in spite of her embracing Christianity, her Mala identity does not disappear. She faces contempt as a Mala and as a Christian woman. As she rightly puts it, there is a Mala well in front of her and Christian pit behind her. All Dalits, whether caste-Dalits or Aboriginals, wear a thorny crown on their head like Vinodini.

This dilemma between her caste and Christian religions brings us back to the parallels in Aboriginal women's writing, although with a significant difference. Here, indigenous religion is as antagonistic towards them as Christianity is in Australia. Vinodini's poem echoes not only her insecurity but also her loss of faith in both religions. She says that the coin of faith that she has been carrying securely in her fist has slipped away somewhere at some point of time. Is she referring to her faith in secularism? Her fear haunts her like a trident, adding religious connotations to her concept of faith. In another poem "The Single Pole Hut," (Vinodini 3-5) she portrays an *agraharam,* an upper caste locality of a village, as she steps into it in search of her upper caste lover. This is the microcosm of Indian society, for she has no place there at all and is thrown away like a "menstrual pad."

Like Australian Aboriginal women writers, Dalit women writers also refuse to dwell on the internal exploitation of women within Dalit societies. For, they speak not as women but as Dalit women. Not many Dalit women writers discuss the exploitation of women within Dalit societies, whereas they are quite vocal about their exploitation outside. It is mostly the urban, educated experience with a certain level of acceptability in society that has been expressed in Dalit women's writing so far rural and remote communities still remaining unknown or invisible. Still the experience and protest of the common Dalit woman in all her poverty, illiteracy and exploitation need to be voiced in literature and compared to, say, Australian example, where they have been voiced. Decisive aspects and experiences of Dalit women as labourers, joginis and sex workers, which are the worst forms of caste and gender discrimination, have not yet really been explored by Dalit women writers. Dalit literature also has gone through and is going through dilemmas and controversies similar to those that Australian Aboriginal literature has faced. For instance, the questions of definition and boundaries of Dalit literature, who should write about Dalits or should others write about Dalits, and so on. Attempts to reconcile and assimilate have but been terrible failures; protests and attempts to alter the existing society naturally influence these two movements and literatures. All these form the core of Dalit literature as they form the basis and essence of Australian Aboriginal literature.

We may, therefore, conclude with some force that (a) Australian Aboriginal women's autobiographical and other writing forms a most significant locus for both a historical study and a responsible social study; (b) comparisons of this body of writing with Australian Aboriginal male writing are bound to throw significant light on the subjects of colonialism and racism within Australia; and (c) comparisons of their predicament and literature with similar predicaments and literatures elsewhere (as in India) may lead to a wider perspective in the general domain of both Aboriginal studies and colonial studies.

Bibliography

Primary Sources

Clare, Monica. *Karobran: The Story of an Aboriginal Girl.* 1978. Chippendale: Alternative Publishing Cooperative, 1987.

Crawford, Evelyn. *Over My Tracks: A Remarkable Life.* Ringwood: Penguin, 1993.

Edmund, Mabel. *No Regrets.* St. Lucia: University of Queensland Press, 1992.

Ginibi, Ruby Langford. *Don't Take Your Love to Town.* Ringwood: Penguin, 1988.

_____. *Real Deadly.* 1992. Sydney: HarperCollins, 1994.

_____. *My Bundjalung People.* St. Lucia: University of Queensland Press, 1994.

Hegarty, Ruth. *Is That You Ruthie?* St. Lucia: University of Queensland Press, 1999.

Huggins, Rita and Jackie Huggins. *Auntie Rita.* 1994. Canberra: Aboriginal Studies Press, 1996.

Kennedy, Marnie. *Born a Half-Caste.* 1985. Canberra: Aboriginal Studies Press, 1990.

Labumore, Elsie Roughsey. *An Aboriginal Mother Tells of the Old and the New.* Fitzroy: McPhee Gribble, 1984.

Morgan, Sally. *My Place.* Fremantle: Fremantle Arts Centre Press, 1987.

Nannup, Alice, Lauren Marsh and Stephen Kinnane. *When the Pelican Laughed.* 1992. South Fremantle: Fremantle Arts Centre Press, 1993.

Simon, Ella. *Through My Eyes.* 1978. Blackburn: Collins Dove, 1987.

Smith, Shirley C. *Mum Shirl: An Autobiography.* Richmond: Heinemann Australia, 1981.

Sykes, Roberta. *Snake Dreaming: Autobiography of a Black Woman*, 3 vols. St Leonards: Allen and Unwin, 1997, 1998, 2000.

Tucker, Margaret. *If Everyone Cared.* 1977. Melbourne: Grosvenor, 1983.

Ward, Glenyse. *Wandering Girl.* Broome: Magabala, 1987.

——. *Unna You Fullas.*.Broome: Magabala, 1991.

West, Ida. *Pride against Prejudice: Reminiscences of a Tasmanian Aborigine.* 1984. Canberra: Australian Institute of Aboriginal Studies, 1987.

Secondary Sources

Ackermann, Jessie. *Australia from a Woman's Point of View.* London: Cassell, 1913.

Allen, Paula Gunn. *The Blind Lion.* Berkeley: Thorp Springs, 1975.

_____. *The Sacred Hoop: Recovering the Feminine in American Indian Traditions.* Boston: Beacon, 1986.

Altman, J.C. Niewenhuysen. *The Economic Status of Australian Aborigines.* Cambridge: Cambridge University Press, 1979.

Anderson, Linda. "At the Threshold of the Self: Women and Autobiography." *Women's Writing: A Challenge to Theory*, ed. Moira Monteith. New York: St. Martin's, 1986: 54-70.

Attwood, Bain. "Portrait of an Aboriginal as an Artist: Sally Morgan and the Construction of Aboriginality." *Australian Historical Studies*, Vol. 25, Number 99, 1992: 302-18.

Bama. *Karukku.* Trans. Lakshmi Holmstrom. Chennai: Macmillan, 2000.

Bandler, Faith. *Wacvie.* Sydney: Rigby, 1977.

_____. *Marani in Australia.* Sydney: Rigby, 1980.

_____. *Welou My Brother.* Sydney: Rigby, 1980.

_____. *Turning the Tide: A Personal History of the Federal Council for the Advancement of Aborigines and Torres Strait Islanders.* Canberra: Aboriginal Studies Press, 1989.

Banks, Olive. *Faces of Feminism.* Oxford: Martin Robertson, 1981.

Barwick, Meening and White, ed. *Fighters and Singers: The Lives of Some Aboriginal Women.* Sydney: Allen and Unwin, 1985.

Basedow, H. *The Australian Aboriginal.* Adelaide: Preece, 1925.

Bates, D. *The Passing of the Aborigines.* Melbourne: Murray, 1938.

Bell, Dianne. *Daughters of the Dreaming.* 1983. Sydney: Allen and Unwin, 1993.

Beniuk, David. "Contemporary Aboriginal Song in a Postcolonial Context." *nlr*, Number 31, Summer 1995: 69-87.

Bennell, Eddie and Anne Thomas. *Aboriginal Legends.* Adelaide: Rigby, 1981.

Benstock, Shari, ed. *The Private Self: Theory and Practice of Women's Autobiographical Writings.* London: The University of North Carolina Press, 1988.

Berndt, Ronald M. and Catherine H. *The World of the First Australians: Aboriginal Traditional Life: Past and Present.* 1964. Canberra: Aboriginal Studies Press, 1992.

_____ *The Speaking Land: Myth and Story in Aboriginal Australia.* Ringwood: Penguin, 1989.

Beverley, John. "The Margin at the Center: On Testimonio (Testimonial Narrative)." *De/Colonising the Subject: The Politics of Gender in Women's Autobiography,* ed. Sidonie Smith and Sam Watson. Minneapolis: University of Minnesota Press, 1992: 91-114.

Bird, Delys and Dennis Haskell, ed. *Whose Place? A Study of Sally Morgan's 'My Place.'* Pymble: Angus and Robertson, 1992.

Blackman, Margaret B. *During My Time: Florence Edenshaw Davidson—A Haida Woman.* 1982. Washington: University of Washington Press, 1992.

Blainley, Geoffrey. *The Triumph of the Nomads.* Melbourne: Macmillan, 1975.

Bleakley, J.W. *The Aborigines of Australia: Their History, Their Habits, Their Assimilation.* Brisbane: Jacaranda Press, 1961.

Bott, E. *Family and Social Network.* London: Tavistock, 1957.

Bowden, Ros and Bill Bunbury. *Being Aboriginal: Comments, Observations and Stories from Aboriginal Australians.* 1990; Sydney: Australian Broadcasting Corporation, 1992.

Brewster, Anne. *Literary Formations: Post-Colonialism, Nationalism, Globalism.* Carlton South: Melbourne University Press, 1995.

_____. *Reading Aboriginal Women's Autobiography.* Sydney: Sydney University Press, 1996.

Brewster, Anne, Angeline O'Neill and Rosemary Van Den Berg, ed. *Those Who Remain Will Always Remember: An Anthology of Aboriginal Writing.* Fremantle: Fremantle Arts Centre Press, 2000.

Brock, Peggy, ed. *Words and Silences: Aboriginal women, politics and land.* Crows Nest: Allen and Unwin, 2001.

Brodzki, Bella and Celeste Schenck. *Life/Lines: Theorising Women's Autobiography.* New York: Cornell University Press, 1988.

Butler, Judith. *Gender Trouble: Feminism and the Subversion of Identity.* New York: Routledge, 1990.

Cameron, Deborah, ed. *The Feminist Critique of Language: A Reader.* London: Routledge, 1990.

Caraway, Nancie. *Segregated Sisterhoods: Racism and the Politics of American Feminism.* Knoxville: University of Tennessee Press, 1991.

Carmody, Kevin. "The Bitter Cake." *Social Alternatives,* Number 1, 1988: 4-5.

Carroll, Rebecca, ed. *I Know What the Red Clay Looks Like: The Voice and Vision of Black Women Writers.* New York: Crown Trade Paperbacks, 1994.

Charlesworth, Max, Howard Morphy, Dianne Bell and Kenneth Maddock, ed. *Religion in Aboriginal Australia.* Brisbane: University of Queensland Press, 1984.

Chesson, Keith, ed. *Jack Davis: A Life Story.* Melbourne: Dent, 1988.

Clark, Manning. *History of Australia.* Melbourne: Melbourne University Press, 1993.

Cockshut, A.D.J. *The Art of Autobiography in 19th and 20th Century England.* London: Yale University Press, 1984.

Cohen, Patsy and Margaret Somerville. *Ingelba and the Five Black Matriarchs.* Sydney: Allen and Unwin, 1990.

Colmer, John. *Australia's Autobiography: The Personal Quest.* Melbourne: OUP, 1982.

Dale, Spender. *Feminist Theories.* London: Women's Press, 1983.

Dangle, Arjun, ed. *Poisoned Bread: Translations from Modern Marathi Dalit Literature.* Hyderabad: Orient Longman, 1992.

Davis J. and B. Hodge. *Aboriginal Writing Today.* Canberra: Aboriginal Studies Press, 1985.

Davis, Jack, Eva Johnson, Richard Walley and Bob Maza. *Plays from Black Australia.* Sydney: Currency Press, 1989.

Davis, Jack, Stephen Muecke, Mudrooroo Narogin and Adam Shoemaker, ed. *Paperbark: A Collection of Black Australian Writings.* St. Lucia: University of Queensland Press, 1990.

Davis, Jack and Adam Shoemaker. "Aboriginal Literature: Written." *Australian Literary Studies,* Vol. 14, Number 3, October 1988: 22-40.

Dawson, James. *Australian Aborigines.* Melbourne: George Robertson, 1881.

Daylight, Phyllis and Mary Johnson. *Women's Business.* Canberra: Australian Government Publishing Service, 1976.

Dixson, Miriam. *The Real Matilda: Woman and Identity in Australia: 1788 to the Present.* Sydney: UNSW Press, 1976.

Docker, John and Gerald Fischer, ed. *Race, Colour and Identity in Australia and New Zealand.* Sydney: UNSW Press, 2000.

Edwards, W.H. *An Introduction to the Aboriginal Societies.* 1988. Wentworth Falls: Social Sciences Press, 1996.

_____. *Traditional Aboriginal Society: A Reader.* Melbourne: Macmillan, 1987.

Einstein, Hester. *Contemporary Feminist Thought.* Sydney: George Allen and Unwin, 1980.

Elkin, A.P. *The Australian Aborigines: how to understand them.* Sydney: Angus and Robertson, 1938.

Emmanuel S. Nelson, ed. *Connections: Essays on Black Literature.* Canberra: Aboriginal Studies Press, 1985.

Evans, Raymonds. "'Don't You Remember Black Alice, Sam Holt?' Aboriginal Women in Queensland History." *HECATE: A Women's Interdisciplinary Journal*, Vol. VIII, Number 2, 1982: 6-21.

Freedman, Diane P. *An Alchemy of Genres: Cross-Genre Writing by American Feminist Poet-Critics.* London: University Press of Virginia, 1992.

Fogarty, Lionell. *Kargun.* Brisbane: Cheryl Buchanan, 1980.

Gale, Fay. *Urban Aborigines.* Canberra: Australian National University, 1972.

_____, ed. *Woman's Role in Aboriginal Society.* Canberra: Australian Institute of Aboriginal Studies, 1974.

_____, ed. *We are Bosses Ourselves.* Canberra: Australian Institute of Aboriginal Studies, 1983.

Gardiner, Judith Kegan. "On Female Identity and Writing by Women." *Writing and Sexual Difference*, ed. Elizabeth Abel. Chicago: University of Chicago Press, 1982: 177-92.

Gilbert, Helen and Joanne Tompkins. *Post-Colonial Drama: Theory, Practice, Politics.* London: Routledge, 1996.

Gilbert, Kevin. *Living Black: Blacks Talk to Kevin Gilbert.* 1977; Ringwood: Penguin, 1978.

_____, ed. *Inside Black Australia: An Anthology of Aboriginal Poetry.* Ringwood: Penguin, 1988.

Ginibi, Ruby Langford and Penny Van Toorn. "Who's in Whose Canon? Transforming Aboriginal Writers into Big Guns." *Southerly: A Review of Australian Literature*, Vol. 57, No. 3, Spring 1997: 125-36.

Glass, Colleen and Archie Weller, ed. *Us Fellas: An Anthology of Aboriginal Writing*. Perth: Artlook, 1987.

Goodwin, Ken. *Macmillan History of Australian Literature.* Melbourne: Macmillan, 1986.

Gordon, Deborah. "Writing Culture, Writing Feminism: The Poetics and Politics of Experimental Ethnography." *Inscriptions*, 3/4, 1988: 7-24.

Grieve, Norma and Patricia Grimshaw, ed. *Australian Women: Feminist Perspectives.* Melbourne: Oxford University Press, 1981.

Harrison, Jane. *Stolen*. Sydney: Currency Press, 1998.

Healy, J.J. *Literature and the Aborigine in Australia.* St. Lucia: University of Queensland Press, 1978.

Heiss, Anita. *Token Koori*. Sydney: Curringa Communications, 1998.

Hergenhan, L.T., ed. *The Penguin New Literary History of Australia.* Ringwood: Penguin, 1988.

Heseltine, Harry, ed. *The Penguin Book of Australian Verse.* Ringwood: Penguin, 1972.

Holt, Lillian. "Testimonio. One Aboriginal Woman's Identity: Walking in Both Worlds." *Australian Feminist Studies*, Number 18, Summer 1993: 175-79.

hooks, bell. *Talking Back: Thinking Feminist, Thinking Black.* Boston: South End Press, 1989.

_____. *Yearning: Race, Gender, and Cultural Politics.* Boston: South End Press, 1990.

Horton, David, ed. *Encyclopaedia of Aboriginal Australia.* CD-ROM, Canberra: Australian Institute for Aboriginal and Torres Strait Islander Studies, 1994.

Howitt, A.W. *The Native Tribes of South-East Australia.* London: Macmillan, 1904.

Huffer, Virginia. *The Sweetness of the Fig: Aboriginal Women in Transition.* Sydney: New South Wales University Press, 1980.

Huggins, Jackie. *Sister Girl: The Writings of Aboriginal Activist and Historian.* St. Lucia: University of Queensland Press, 1998.

_____. "Always Was and Always Will Be." *Australian Historical Studies,* Vol. 25, Number 100, 1993: 459-64.

Janson, Julie. *Black Mary* and *Gunjies*. Canberra: Aboriginal Studies Press, 1996.

Jelinck, Estelle C., ed. *Women's Autobiographies: Essays in Criticism*. Bloomington: Indiana University Press, 1980.

Jennings, Karen. *Sites of Difference: Cinematic Representations of Aboriginality and Gender, The Moving Image*, Number 1. Melbourne: Australian Film Institute, 1993.

Kapetas, Jan Teagle et al, ed. *From Our Hearts: An Anthology of New Aboriginal Writing from Southwest Western Australia.* South Fremantle: Kadadjiny Mia Walyalup Writers, 2000.

Keen, Ian. *Being Black*. Canberra: Aboriginal Studies Press, 1994.

Klein, Viola. *The Feminine Character: History of an Ideology*. London: Routledge and Kegan Paul, 1946.

Krausmann, Rudi, ed. *Long Water: Aboriginal Art and Literature*. Bathurst: Robert Brown, 1988.

Krupat, Arnold. *The Voice in the Margin: Native American Literature and the Canon*. Los Angeles: University of California Press, 1989.

Lambert, Johanna. *Wise Women of the Dreamtime: Aboriginal Tales of the Ancestral Powers*. Vermont: Inner Traditions International, 1993.

Lawson, A. "Comparative studies and postcolonial 'settler' cultures." *Australian-Canadian Studies*, Vol. 10, Number 2, 1991: 153-59.

Leach, B., ed. *The Aborigines Today*. Melbourne: Paul Hamlyn, 1971.

Leavitt, Rohrlich, ed. *Women Cross-Culturally: Change and Challenge*. The Hague: Mouton, 1975.

Lionnet, Francoise. *Autobiographical Voices: Race, Gender, Self-Portraiture*. London: Cornell University Press, 1989.

_____. "Autoethnography: The An-Archic Style of *Dust Tracks on a Road*." *Autobiographical Voices: Race, Gender, Self-Portraiture*. New York: Cornell University Press, 1989: 97-129

Lippman, Lorna. *Generations of Resistance: Mabo and Justice*. 1981. Melbourne: Longman Cheshire, 1994.

Lumholtz, C. *Among Cannibals*. London: Murray, 1889.

Mackenzie, Norman. *Women in Australia*. Melbourne: Cheshire, 1962.

Maddock, Kenneth. *The Australian Aborigines: A Portrait of Their Society*. London: Penguin, 1974.

Maris, Hyllus and Sonia Borg. *Women of the Sun*. Victoria: Penguin, 1985.

McConnell, U.H. "Mourning rituals among the tribes of Cape York Peninsula." *Oceania,* Vol. VII, No. 3, 1937: 346-48.

McCooey, David. *Artful Histories: Modern Australian Autobiography.* Melbourne: Cambridge University Press, 1996.

McLaren, John. *Australian Literature: An Historical Introduction.* Melbourne: Longman Cheshire, 1989.

McLaren, Philip. *Sweet Water—Stolen Land.* Queensland: University of Queensland Press, 1993.

Medcraft, Rosalie and Valda Gee. *The Sausage Tree.* St. Lucia: University of Queensland Press, 1995.

Minh-ha, Trinh T. *Woman, Native and the Other: Writing Postcoloniality and Feminism.* Bloomington: Indiana University Press, 1989.

Mitchell, Juliet and Ann Oakley, ed. *What is Feminism?* New York: Pantheon, 1986.

Moffett, James. *Teaching the Universe of Discourse.* Boston: Houghton Mifflin, 1968.

Moi, Toril. *Sexual/Textual Politics: Feminist Literary Theory.* London: Methuen, 1985.

Moreton-Robinson, Aileen. *Talkin' up to the White Woman:.Indigenous Women and Feminism.* St. Lucia: University of Queensland Press, 2000.

Moriarty, John. *Saltwater Fella.* Ringwood: Penguin Australia, 2000.

Mudrooroo. *Us Mob: History, Culture, Struggle: An Introduction to Indigenous Australia.* 1995. Sydney: HarperCollins, 2001.

_____ *Indigenous Literature of Australia: Milli Milli Wangka.* Melbourne: Hyland, 1997.

Muecke, Stephen. "Aboriginal Literature and the Repressive Hypothesis." *Southerly: A Review of Australian Literature*, XLVIII, No. 4, 1988: 405-18.

Nalson, J. Usury. *From Tribal Brotherhood to Universal Otherhood.* Chicago: Chicago University Press, 1965.

Narogin, Mudrooroo. *Dalwurra: The Black Bittern.* Perth: University of Western Australia, 1988.

_____. *Writing from the Fringe: A Study of Modern Aboriginal Literature.* Melbourne: Hyland House, 1990.

Newman, Joan. "Commitment and Constraint: Contemporary Koori Writing." *From a Distance: Australian Writers and Cultural Displacement.* Ommundsen, Wenche and Hazel Rowley, ed. Geelong: Deakin University Press, 1996: 83-91.

_____. "Reader-Response to Transcribed Oral Narrative: *A Fortunate Life* and *My Place*." *Southerly: A Review of Australian Literature*, XLVIII, No. 4, 1988: 376-89.

Ngûgî, wa Thiong'o. *Decolonising the Mind: the Politics of Language in African Literature.* 1986. Harare: Zimbabwe Publishing House, 1987.

Noonuccal, Oodgeroo. *We Are Going*. Brisbane: Jacaranda Press, 1964.

_____. *The Dawn is at Hand.* Brisbane: Jacaranda Press, 1966.

_____. *My People.* Brisbane: Jacaranda Press, 1970.

_____. *Stradbroke Dreamtime.* Sydney: Angus and Robertson, 1972.

_____. *Father Sky and Mother Earth.* Queensland: Jacaranda Press, 1981.

Nyoongah, Mudrooroo. *Aboriginal Mythology: An A-Z spanning the history of the Australian Aboriginal people from the earliest legends to the present day.* California: Aquarian, 1994.

Olney, James. *Metaphors of Self: The Meaning of Autobiography.* Princeton: Princeton University Press, 1972.

_____, ed. *Autobiography: Essays Theoretical and Critical.* Princeton: Princeton University Press, 1980.

O'Shane, Pat. "Sin of Omission." *The Weekend Australian*, November 7-8, 1998: 29.

Paisley, Fiona. *Loving Protection? Australian Feminism and Women's Rights, 1919-1939.* Carlton South: Melbourne University Press, 2000.

Parsons, Nick. *Dead Heart.* Sydney: Currency Press, 1996.

Payne, S. "Aboriginal Women and the Criminal Justice System." *Aboriginal Law Bulletin*, Vol. 2, No. 46, October 1990: 9-11

Perkins, Charles. *A Bastard like Me.* Sydney: Ure Smith, 1975.

Perry, Donna. *Blacktalk: Women Writers Speak Out.* New Jersey: Rutgers University Press, 1990.

Pettman, Jan. *Living in the Margins: Racism, Sexism and Feminism in Australia.* St. Leonards: Allen and Unwin, 1992.

Rajkowski, Pamela. *Linden Girl*: A *Story of Outlawed Lives.* Nedlands: University of Western Australia Press, 1995.

Rani, Challapalli Swaroopa. "A Forbidden History." Trans. K. Damodar Rao. *Indian Literature*, 200, Nov.-Dec. 2000: 91-92.

Reagon, Bernice Johnson. "My Black Mothers and Sisters or On Beginning a Cultural Autobiography." *Feminist Studies*, Number 8, Spring 1982: 81-96.

Reed, A.W. *Aboriginal Stories of Australia*. 1980. Sydney: Reed New Holland, 1998.

_____. *Aboriginal Myths: Tales of the Dreamtime*. 1982. Sydney: Reed New Holland, 1999.

Reed-Gilbert, Kerry. Comp. *The Strength of Us as Women: Black Women Speak*. Charnwood: Ginninderra Press, 2000.

Reynolds, Henry. *Fate of a Free People: A Radical Re-Examination of the Tasmanian Wars*. Ringwood: Penguin Australia, 1995.

Rigg, Julie, ed. *In Her Own Right*. Melbourne: Thomas Nelson, 1969.

Rose, Debora Bird. *Hidden Histories: Black Stories from Victoria River Downs, Humbert River and Wave Hill Stations*. Canberra: Aboriginal Studies Press, 1991.

Roth, W.E. *Ethnological studies among the north-west-central Queensland Aborigines*. Brisbane: Government Printer, 1897.

Rowley, C.D. *Outcasts in White Australia*. Harmondsworth: Penguin, 1972.

_____. *The Destruction of Aboriginal Society*. Canberra: Australian University Press, 1970.

Ruffo, Armand Garnet, ed. *(Ad)dressing Our Words: Aboriginal Perspectives on Aboriginal Literatures*. Penticton: Theytus, 2001.

Rutherford, Anna, ed. *Aboriginal Culture Today*. Sydney: Dangaroo Press, 1988.

Schaffer, Kay. *Women and the Bush: Forces of Desire in the Australian Cultural Tradition*. Cambridge: Cambridge University Press, 1988.

Schneir, Miriam, ed. *Feminism: The Essential Historical Writings*. New York: Vintage, 1972.

Scott, John. "Aboriginal Theatre: Does 'Sold Out' mean 'Selling Out'?" *Race and Class*, Vol. 35, No. 4, 1994: 107-11.

Shoemaker, Adam. *Black Words; White Page: Aboriginal Literature 1929-1988*. St. Lucia: University of Queensland Press, 1989.

Showalter, Elaine. "Feminist Criticism in the Wilderness." *The New Feminist Criticism: Essays on Women, Literature, and Theory*, ed. Elaine Showalter. New York: Pantheon, 1985: 243-70.

Smith, L.R. *The Aboriginal Population of Australia*. Canberra: A.N.U. Press, 1980.

Smith, Sidonie. *Subjectivity, Identity, and the Body: Women's Autobiographical Practices in the Twentieth Century*. Bloomington: Indiana University Press, 1993.

Smith, Sidonie and Julia Watson, ed. *De/Colonising the Subject: The Politics in Women's Autobiography.* Minneapolis: University of Minnesota Press, 1992.

Smith, Valerie. "Black Feminist Theory and the Representation of the 'Other'." *Changing Our Own Words: Essays in Criticism, Theory and Writing by Black Women,* ed. Cheryl A. Wall. New Brunswick: Rutgers University Press, 1989: 38-57.

Smith, William Ramsay. *Aborigine: Myths and Legends.* London: Random House, 1996.

Spivak, Gayatri Chakravorty. "Identity and Alterity—An Interview with Nikos Papastergiadis." *Arena,* Summer 1997: 65-76.

Stanley, Sandra Kumamoto, ed. *Other Sisterhoods: Literary Theory and U.S. Women of Color.* Chicago: University of Illinois Press, 1998.

Stewart, Margaret. *Ngalengangpum jarrakpu purrurn: Mother and Child.* Broome: Magabala, 1999.

Summers, Anne. *Damned Whores and God's Police: The Colonisation of Women in Australia.* Ringwood: Penguin, 1975.

Sykes, Roberta. Personal interview. 9 January 1998.

Tatz, Colin. *Black Viewpoints.* Sydney: Australian and New Zealand Book Co., 1975.

Taylor, Alf. *Winds.* Broome: Magabala, 1994.

_____. *Long Time Now: stories of the dreamtime, the here and now.* Broome: Magabala, 2001.

Themann, H.E. and Buludja, B. *Tell the White Man.* Sydney: Collins, 1949.

Tillie, Olsen. *Silences.* London: Virago, 1980.

Tindale, N.B. *Aboriginal Tribes of Australia.* Berkeley: University of California Press, 1974.

Trees, Kathryn and Colin Johnson. "Postcolonialism: Yet another Colonial Strategy?" *Span,* Vol. 1, Number 36, 1993: 264-65.

Tugby, D. *Aboriginal Identity in Contemporary Australian Society.* Brisbane: Jacaranda Press, 1973.

Turcotte, Gerry, ed. *Writers in Action: The Writer's Choice Evenings.* Sydney: Currency Press, 1990.

_____, ed. *Jack Davis: The Maker of History.* Sydney: Angus and Robertson, 1994.

Vinodini. "The Single Pole Hut," trans. K. Suneetha Rani. *Chandrabhaga,* Number 2, 2000: 3-5.

Walker, Shirley, ed. *Who is She? Images of Women in Australian Fiction.* St. Lucia: University of Queensland Press, 1983.

Wandor, Michelene. "Voices are Wild." *Women's Writing: A Challenge to Theory*, ed. Moira Monteith. New York: St. Martin's, 1986: 72-89.

Warlpiri Women's Voices: Our Lives Our History. Alice Springs: IAD Press, 1995.

Warner, W.L. *A Black Civilization: A Study of an Australian Aboriginal Tribe.* New York: Harper, 1958.

Weare, Ramayne. *Malanbarra.* Broome: Magabala, 1997.

Weller, Archie. *The Day of the Dog.* St. Leonards: Allen and Unwin, 1981.

Whitlock, Gillian. *The Intimate Empire: Reading Women's Autobiography.* London: Cassell, 2000.

Williams, Magdalene, ed. *Ngay janijirr ngank: This is My Word.* Broome: Magabala, 1999.

Windschuttle, Elizabeth, ed. *Women, Class and History.* Melbourne: Fontana, 1980.

Woods, J.D. *The Native Tribes of South Australia.* Adelaide: Wigg, 1879.

Wright, Alexis. *Plains of Promise.* Queensland: Queensland University Press, 2000.